CW01667038

COLLECT

Apart from six wartime years in the Royal Navy, Charles Causley has lived all his life at Launceston, in Cornwall, where he also worked for many years as a teacher. In 1967 he received the Queen's Gold Medal for Poetry and in 1986 was appointed CBE. In 1990 he was the recipient of the prestigious Ingersoll/T.S. Eliot Award, given to authors 'of abiding importance whose work affirms the moral principles of Western civilisation.'

By the same author

POEMS

Farewell, Aggie Weston
Survivor's Leave
Union Street
Johnny Alleluia
Underneath the Water
Figure of 8: Narrative Poems
Figgie Hobbin
The Hill of the Fairy Calf
The Animals' Carol
Secret Destinations
Early in the Morning
Jack the Treacle Eater
A Field of Vision
The Young Man of Cury

VERSE PLAYS

The Gift of a Lamb
The Ballad of Aucassin and Nicolette

TRANSLATION

25 Poems by Hamdija Demirović

SHORT STORIES

Hands to Dance and Skylark

CHILDREN'S STORIES

The Tail of the Trinosaur (in verse)
Dick Whittington
Three Heads Made of Gold
The Last King of Cornwall

AS EDITOR

Peninsula
Dawn and Dusk
Rising Early
Modern Folk Ballads
The Puffin Book of Magic Verse
The Puffin Book of Salt-Sea Verse
The Batsford Book of Story Poems
The Sun, Dancing

Charles Causley

COLLECTED POEMS

M
PAPERMAC

Copyright © Charles Causley 1951, 1953, 1957, 1961, 1968, 1969, 1970, 1975, 1981, 1984, 1986, 1987, 1988, 1991, 1992

All rights reserved. No reproduction, copy or transmission of this publication may be made without written permission. No paragraph of this publication may be reproduced, copied or transmitted save with written permission or in accordance with the provisions of the Copyright Act 1956 (as amended). Any person who does any unauthorised act in relation to this publication may be liable to criminal prosecution and civil claims for damages.

The right of Charles Causley to be identified as author of this work has been asserted by him in accordance with the Copyright, Designs and Patents Act 1988.

First published in hardback 1992 by
MACMILLAN LONDON LIMITED
a division of Pan Macmillan Publishers Limited
Cavaye Place London SW10 9PG
and Basingstoke
and simultaneously in paperback by
PAPERMAC

Associated companies in Auckland, Budapest, Dublin, Gaborone, Harare, Hong Kong, Kampala, Kuala Lumpur, Lagos, Madras, Manzini, Melbourne, Mexico City, Nairobi, New York, Singapore, Sydney, Tokyo and Windhoek

3 8 7 9 8 6 4

ISBN 0-333-57516-4 (hardback)
ISBN 0-333-57517-2 (paperback)

A CIP catalogue record for this book is available from the British Library

Phototypeset by Intype, London
Printed and bound in Great Britain by
Makays of Chatham PLC, Chatham, Kent

NOTE

This book contains all those of my poems I wish to preserve. Poetry, however unlikely its subject, theme or surface appearance, has always been to me a particular form of autobiography. The temptation, for whatever reason, to re-cast or rewrite certain earlier poems when preparing a collected edition seems best resisted. Rather, I choose to omit such work altogether, or let it stand with the rest as representative of a certain time and place and attitude of mind: the imaginative energy thus saved, perhaps, more usefully employed in writing something entirely new.

The present *Collected Poems* represents work from my *Collected Poems 1951–75* (Macmillan, 1975), *The Ballad of Aucassin and Nicolette* (Kestrel, 1981), *Secret Destinations* (Macmillan, 1984), *Early in the Morning* (Viking Kestrel, 1986), *Jack the Treacle Eater* (Macmillan, 1987), *A Field of Vision* (Macmillan, 1988) and *The Young Man of Cury* (Macmillan, 1991). Other poems are hitherto uncollected or appear for the first time.

Launceston
Cornwall

C.C.

CONTENTS

KEATS AT TEIGNMOUTH

Spring 1818

BY THE wild sea-wall I wandered
  Blinded by the salting sun,
While the sulky Channel thundered
  Like an old Trafalgar gun.

And I watched the gaudy river
  Under trees of lemon-green,
Coiling like a scarlet bugle
  Through the valley of the Teign.

When spring fired her fusilladoes
  Salt-spray, sea-spray on the sill,
When the budding scarf of April
  Ravelled on the Devon hill,

Then I saw the crystal poet
  Leaning on the old sea-rail;
In his breast lay death, the lover,
  In his head, the nightingale.

A BALLAD FOR KATHARINE OF ARAGON

Queen of England, 1509–1533
Buried in Peterborough Cathedral

As I walked down by the river
Down by the frozen fen
I saw the grey cathedral
With the eyes of a child of ten.
O the railway arch is smoky
As the Flying Scot goes by
And but for the Education Act
Go Jumper Cross and I.

But war is a bitter bugle
That all must learn to blow
And it didn't take long to stop the song
In the dirty Italian snow.
O war is a casual mistress
And the world is her double bed.
She has a few charms in her mechanised arms
But you wake up and find yourself dead.

The olive tree in winter
Casts her banner down
And the priest in white and scarlet
Comes up from the muddy town.
O never more will Jumper
Watch the Flying Scot go by.
His funeral knell was a six-inch shell
Singing across the sky.

The Queen of Castile has a daughter
Who won't come home again.
She lies in the grey cathedral
Under the arms of Spain.
O the Queen of Castile has a daughter
Torn out by the roots,
Her lovely breast in a cold stone chest
Under the farmers' boots.

Now I like a Spanish party
And many O many's the day
I have watched them swim as the night came dim
In Algeciras Bay.
O the high sierra was thunder
And the seven-branched river of Spain
Came down to the sea to plunder
The heart of the sailor again.

O shall I leap in the river
And knock upon paradise door
For a gunner of twenty-seven and a half
And a queen of twenty-four?
From the almond tree by the river
I watch the sky with a groan,
For Jumper and Kate are always out late
And I lie here alone.

party: girl (naval slang)

NURSERY RHYME
OF
INNOCENCE AND EXPERIENCE

I HAD a silver penny
  And an apricot tree
And I said to the sailor
  On the white quay

'Sailor O sailor
  Will you bring me
If I give you my penny
  And my apricot tree

'A fez from Algeria
  An Arab drum to beat
A little gilt sword
  And a parakeet?'

And he smiled and he kissed me
  As strong as death
And I saw his red tongue
  And I felt his sweet breath

'*You may keep your penny*
  And your apricot tree
And I'll bring your presents
  Back from sea.'

O the ship dipped down
  On the rim of the sky
And I waited while three
  Long summers went by

Then one steel morning
  On the white quay
I saw a grey ship
  Come in from sea

Slowly she came
  Across the bay
For her flashing rigging
  Was shot away

All round her wake
  The seabirds cried
And flew in and out
  Of the hole in her side

Slowly she came
  In the path of the sun
And I heard the sound
  Of a distant gun

And a stranger came running
  Up to me
From the deck of the ship
  And he said, said he

'O are you the boy
  Who would wait on the quay
With the silver penny
  And the apricot tree?

'I've a plum-coloured fez
  And a drum for thee
And a sword and a parakeet
  From over the sea.'

'O where is the sailor
  With bold red hair?
And what is that volley
  On the bright air?

'O where are the other
  Girls and boys?
And why have you brought me
  Children's toys?'

SONG OF THE DYING GUNNER AA1

OH MOTHER my mouth is full of stars
As cartridges in the tray
My blood is a twin-branched scarlet tree
And it runs all runs away.

Oh 'Cooks to the galley' is sounded off
And the lads are down in the mess
But I lie done by the forrard gun
With a bullet in my breast.

Don't send me a parcel at Christmas time
Of socks and nutty and wine
And don't depend on a long weekend
By the Great Western Railway line.

Farewell, Aggie Weston, the Barracks at Guz,
Hang my tiddley suit on the door
I'm sewn up neat in a canvas sheet
And I shan't be home no more.

[HMS *Glory*]

AA1: Anti-Aircraft Gunner, 1st Class
Aggie Weston: the familiar term used by sailors to describe the hostels founded in many seaports by Dame Agnes Weston
Guz: naval slang for Devonport
tiddley suit: sailor's best shore-going uniform with gold badges

HMS *GLORY*

I WAS born on an Irish sea of eggs and porter,
I was born in Belfast, in the MacNeice country,
A child of Harland & Wolff in the iron forest,
My childbed a steel cradle slung from a gantry.

I remember the Queen's Road trams swarming with
workers,
The lovely northern voices, the faces of the women,
The plane trees by the City Hall: an *Alexanderplatz*,
And the sailors coming off shore with silk stockings
and linen.

I remember the jokes about sabotage and Dublin,
The noisy jungle of cranes and sheerlegs, the clangour,
The draft in February of a thousand matelots from
Devonport,
Surveying anxiously my enormous flight-deck and
hangar.

I remember the long vista of ships under the quiet
mountain,
The signals from Belfast Castle, the usual panic and
sea-fever
Before I slid superbly out on the green lough
Leaving the tiny cheering figures on the jetty for ever:

Turning my face from home to the Southern Cross,
A map of crackling stars, and the albatross.

HMS *GLORY* AT SYDNEY

August 1945

Now it seems an old forgotten fable:
The snow goose descending on the still lagoon,
The trees of summer flowering ice and fire
And the sun coming up on the Blue Mountains.

But I remember, I remember Sydney,
Our bows scissoring the green cloth of the sea,
Prefaced by plunging dolphins we approached her:
The land of the kookaburra and the eucalyptus tree.

The harbour bridge, suddenly sketched by Whistler,
Appeared gently on a horizon of smudges and pearls,
And the sun came up behind us
With a banging of drums from the Solomons.

O! I shall never forget you on that crystal morning!
Your immense harbour, your smother of deep green
trees,
The skyscrapers, waterfront shacks, parks and
radio-towers,
And the tiny pilot-boat, the *Captain Cook*,
Steaming to meet us:
Our gallery deck fringed with the pale curious faces
of sailors
Off the morning watch.

O like maidens preparing for the court ball
We pressed our number-one suits,
Borrowing electric irons and starching prim white
collars,
And stepped forth into the golden light
With Australian pound notes in our pockets.

O there is no music
Like the music of the Royal Marine bugler
Sounding off 'Liberty men'.
And there is no thrill
Like stepping ashore in a new country
With a clean shirt and with pound notes in your pocket.

O Sydney, how can I celebrate you
Sitting here in Cornwall like an old maid
With a bookful of notes and old letters?

I remember the circular bar in Castlereagh Street
And the crowds of friendly Aussies with accents like
  tin-openers,
Fighting for schooners of onion beer.
I remember Janie, magnificent, with red hair,
Dressed in black, with violets on her reliable bosom,
Remembering a hundred names and handling the beer
  engines
With the grace and skill of ten boxers.

O Janie, have the races at Melbourne seen you this year?
And do matelots, blushing, still bring you flowers?
Across three continents: across monsoon, desert, jungle,
  city,
Across flights of rare birds in burning Africa,
Across crowds of murderous pilgrims struggling grimly to
  Mecca,
Across silver assaults of flying-fish in the Arabian Sea,
I salute you and your city.

I remember the deep canyons of streets, the great shafts
  of sunlight
Striking on fruit-shop, flower-shop, tram and bookstall,
The disappearing cry of the Underground Railway,
The films: *Alexander Nevsky* and *Salome*,
The plays: *Macbeth* and *Noah* in North Sydney,
And travelling there, across the fantastic bridge,
Our ship, the *Glory*, a lighted beetle,
A brilliant sarcophagus far below
On the waterfront at Woolloomoolloo.

Oh yes, I remember Woolloomoolloo,
The slums with wrought-iron balconies
Upon which one expected to find, asleep in a deckchair,
Asleep in the golden sun, fat, grotesque and belching:
Captain Cook.

The Chinese laundries, the yellow children in
  plum-coloured brocade,
The way they fried the eggs, the oysters and champagne.
I remember Daphne and Lily, the black-market gin,
And crawling back to the docks as the dawn
Cracked on my head.

O the museum with the gigantic, terrifying kangaroo,
Who lived, as huge as a fairy story,
Only ten thousand years ago.

O the sheepskin coats, the woollen ties,
And our wanderings in David Jones' store
Among a rubble of silk stockings and tins of fruit salad.
The books I bought at Angus & Robertson's bookshop,
Sir Osbert Sitwell, and Q (to remind me of home).

I remember the ships and ferries at Circular Quay,
And the tram ride to Botany Bay,
So magnificently like the postage stamp
I bought as a child.
I remember the enormous jail at La Perouse,
The warders on the walls with their rifles.
I remember the Zoo at Taronga Park,
The basking shark I gazed down at in terror,
And the shoes I wore out walking, walking.

And so I celebrate this southern city
To which I shall never return.
I celebrate her fondly, as an old lover,
And I celebrate the names and faces of my companions:

George Swayne, Ron Brunt, Joney,
Tug Wilson, Jan Love, Reg Gilmore,
Pony Moor, Derby Kelly, Mac,

Where are they now?

Now it seems an old forgotten fable:
The snow goose descending on the still lagoon,
The trees of summer flowering ice and fire
And the sun coming up on the Blue Mountains.

HMS *ECLIPSE* APPROACHES FREETOWN

September 1940

I SING of the keen destroyer
Banging on the silken doors of the morning,
Cutting through the panels of the South Atlantic:
Strands of light streaming in the steel rigging.
And the warning:
The yellow stammer from the lighthouse of white sugar
Pales as the African sun unfolds her tail of golden
  peacock
Over the fevered harbour.

Borne on the lusty tide
Past mountains deep and green as Victorian postcards,
My iron mistress, my rusty virgin
Carries me into Sierra Leone, under the lion mountain:
The land of the violet lightning and the thunderstorms
  of sheet iron,
The hills, rich and bursting with the brown and orange
  of Gauguin.
And, in the distance, the blue Sugar Loaf
Wears decently her conventional mists.

CONVOY

DRAW the blanket of ocean
Over the frozen face.
He lies, his eyes quarried by glittering fish,
Staring through the green freezing sea-glass
At the Northern Lights.

He is now a child in the land of Christmas:
Watching, amazed, the white tumbling bears
And the diving seal.
The iron wind clangs round the ice-caps,
The five-pointed Dog-star
Burns over the silent sea,

And the three ships
Come sailing in.

CHIEF PETTY OFFICER

HE IS older than the naval side of British history,
And sits
More permanent than the spider in the enormous
  wall.
His barefoot, coal-burning soul
Expands, puffs like a toad, in the convict air
Of the Royal Naval Barracks at Devonport.

Here, in depot, is his stone Nirvana:
More real than the opium pipes,
The uninteresting relics of his Edwardian foreign
  commission.
And, from his thick stone box,
He surveys with a prehistoric eye the hostilities-only
  ratings.

He has the face of the dinosaur
That sometimes stares from old Victorian naval
  photographs:
That of some elderly lieutenant
With boots and a celluloid Crippen collar,
Brass buttons and cruel ambitious eyes of almond.

He was probably made a Freemason in Hong Kong.
He has a son (on War Work) in the Dockyard,
And an appalling daughter
In the WRNS.
He writes on your draft-chit,
Tobacco permit or request-form
In a huge antique Borstal hand,
And pins notices on the board in the Chiefs' Mess
Requesting his messmates not to
Lay on the billiard table.
He is an anti-Semite, and has somewhat reactionary
  views,
And reads the pictures in the daily news.

And when you return from the nervous Pacific
Where the seas
Shift like sheets of plate-glass in the dazzling
  morning;
Or when you return
Browner than Alexander, from Malta,
Where you have leaned over the side, in harbour,
And seen in the clear water
The salmon-tins, wrecks and tiny explosions of
  crystal fish,
A whole war later
He will still be sitting under a pusser's clock
Waiting for tot-time,
His narrow forehead ruffled by the Jutland wind.

pusser's: strictly naval; naval issue

ELIZABETHAN SAILOR'S SONG

MY LOVE my love is a green box-tree
  And the scarlet hawthorn berry
Give me five cocky starlings on a grass-grown sea
  And a lute to be merry.

Then shall we wander in star-strewn meadows
  Frosted by ancient October
Where ice like iron rims the shadows,
  And never be sober.

O what is the brightness behind her eye?
  O let me taste her sweet mouth, begin,
As under the sky we freezing lie.
  Cold it is out but not within.

O cease your singing my darling my swallow
  And put away your brown fiddle
For the ship is a-sailing and you cannot follow
  And I have the middle.

middle: middle watch; midnight–4 a.m.

CONVERSATION IN GIBRALTAR

1943

We sit here, talking of Barea and Lorca,
Meeting the iron eye of the Spanish clock.
We have cut, with steel bows, the jungle of salt water,
Sustaining the variable sea-fevers of home and women
To walk the blazing ravine
Of the profitable Rock.

We hold, in our pockets, no comfortable return
  tickets:
Only the future, gaping like some hideous fable.
The antique Mediterranean of history and Alexander,
The rattling galley and the young Greek captains
Are swept up and piled
Under the table.

We have walked to Europa and looked east to the
  invisible island,
The bitter rock biting the heel through the shoe-leather.
Rain's vague infantry, the Levant, parachutes on the
  stone lion
And soon, soon, under our feet and the thin steel deck
We shall be conscious of miles of perpendicular sea,
And Admiralty weather.

Admiralty weather: bad weather

RATTLER MORGAN

Now his eyes are bright farthings
  And he spindles
In seas deeper than death.
  His lips are no longer wet with wine
But gleam with green salt
  And the Gulf Stream is his breath.

Now he is fumbled by ancient tides
  Among decks flagged with seaweed
But no flags sees he there.
  His fingers are washed to stone
And to phosphor
  And there are starfish in his hair.

[HMS *Cabbala*]

DEMOBILISATION LEAVE

I HAVE seen the white tiger,
Imagination,
In the Douanier Rousseau forest:
Isosceles leaves and a waterfall of compasses.
And although I am writing in Cornwall, in winter,
And the rain is coming in from the moor,
Trincomali, ah, Trincomali!
The Technicolor market, the monkeys and
  chickens,
The painted boats at Vegetable Jetty,
The rattling lizard and the bored crow
In the burning graveyard:

Here lies David Kelly, Naval Stores Officer,
Died of the Fever,
1816.

O the drums and the pythons and the trick of the
  mango tree,
The warrior Buddha with the brandished sword,
The rosewood elephants and the porcupine
  cigarette boxes.
O the fire opal, zircon and water sapphire,
And the warm beer and peanuts in the P.O.'s
  canteen.
The Chinese cafés, and the rickshaw-boys
Grinning and gambling by the fishmarket.
The rings from Kandy and the black ivory elephants
Crossing the eternal bridge for the mantelshelves
Of thousands and thousands of sailors.

And the carrier and her exhausted planes
Lying in the oily harbour,
'Hands to bathe'
And the liberty-boats
Buzzing over the water.

O the sickly lime-juice at Elephant House
And the cooking that looks of the West
But tastes, O tastes of the East.

And they say:
'You must be fed up with your leave,
Fifty-six days is a long time,
You'll start work before it's over—
You'll be tired of nothing to do,
Nothing to think of,
Nothing to write about.
Yes: you'll go back to the office
Soon.'

AUTOBIOGRAPHY

NOW THAT my sea-going self-possession wavers
I sit and write the letter you will not answer.
The razor at my wrist patiently severs
Passion from thought, of which the flesh is censor.
I walk by the deep canal where moody lovers
Find their Nirvana on each other's tongues,
And in my naked bed the usual fevers
Invade the tropic sense, brambling the lungs.
I am drowned to the sound of seven flooding rivers,
The distant Bombay drum and the *ghazel* dancer,
But the English Sunday, monstrous as India, shivers,
And the voice of the muezzin is the voice of the station
  announcer.
The wet fields blot the bitterness of the cry,
And I turn from the tactful friend to the candid sky.

AT THE GRAVE OF JOHN CLARE

WALKING in the scythed churchyard, around the locked church,
Walking among the oaks and snails and mossed inscriptions
At first we failed to find the grave.
But a girl said, 'There he is: there is John Clare.'
And we stood, silent, by the ridged stone,
A stone of grey cheese.
There were no flowers for the dead ploughman
As the gilt clock fired off the hour,
Only the words:
A poet is born not made.

The dove-grey village lay in the Dutch landscape:
The level-crossing and the fields of wet barley,
The almshouses, the school, the Ebenezer Chapel,
The two pubs, and the signposts
To Stamford, To Maxey
From the pages of biography.
And later, sitting in the church
Among the unstuffed hassocks,
And smoking a pipe on the gate
At Maxey Crossing,
I thought of the dead poet:

Of the books and letters in the Peterborough Museum,
The huge, mad writing.
Of the way he walked, with one foot in the furrow,
Or hurried, terrified, as a child to fetch the flour from Maxey
Expecting from every turn a Caliban.
Of London, Charles Lamb and Hazlitt,
The bad grammar, the spelling, the invented words,
And the poetry bursting like a diamond bomb.
I thought of the last days, the old man
Sitting alone in the porch of All Saints' in Northampton,
And the dead poet trundling home to Helpston.

O Clare! Your poetry clear, translucent
As your lovely name,
I salute you with tears.
And, coming out on the green from the Parting Pot,
I notice a bicycle tyre
Hanging from the high stone feathers of your
monument.

RETURN TO CORNWALL

I THINK no longer of the antique city
  Of Pompey and the red-haired Alexander.
The brilliant harbour, the wrecked light at Pharos,
  Are buried deep with Mediterranean plunder.

Here, by the Inny, nature has her city:
  (O the cypress trees of Mahomed Ali Square!)
The children build their harbour in the meadow
  And the crystal lark floats on the Cornish air.

KING'S COLLEGE CHAPEL

WHEN TO the music of Byrd or Tallis,
  The ruffed boys singing in the blackened stalls,
The candles lighting the small bones on their faces,
  The Tudors stiff in marble on the walls,

There comes to evensong Elizabeth or Henry,
  Rich with brocade, pearl, golden lilies, at the altar,
The scarlet lions leaping on their bosoms,
  Pale royal hands fingering the crackling psalter,

Henry is thinking of his lute and of backgammon,
  Elizabeth follows the waving song, the mystery,
Proud in her red wig and green jewelled favours;
  They sit in their white lawn sleeves, as cool as history.

YELVERTON

I MET her by the Rifle Range
  Among the spent cartridges and the heather.
Gay she was as a pin-table
  And a voice like a loudhailer.

I was stationed in Devonport at the time
  Among the jolly stokers, the yellow-faced
Dark-haired sick-bay tiffies, the Mongolian Chief Yeomen.
  And, for quiet, I came out on a bus to the moor.

Here, by the church of battleship grey,
  The auctioneers' advertisements, the sound of water,
Among the lovely ponies and the fat golfers
  I met her by the Rifle Range.

And so, when peace came, I never returned to Glasgow.
  Now I work as a fitter in the dockyard
And, I might say, as an ex-service man
  I was lucky to get the job.

We've a nice little place here at Yelverton,
  And although it's a bit chilly in winter
There's plenty of room on the moor for the kiddies
  And we have nice little outings to Princetown.

All the same, I am sure you will see
  Why I do not wish to join the Rifle Club?
Myself, on the long winter evenings,
  I find myself thinking of the Royal Naval Barracks at
    Devonport:

Remembering the jolly stokers, the yellow-faced
  Dark-haired sick-bay tiffies, the Mongolian Chief Yeomen,
And, behind the backcloth of cranes and acetylene welders,
  The splendid sea.

sick-bay tiffies: sick-berth attendants.

LEGEND

As I walked over the western plain
  The silent snow descending
I saw winter lean on the valley's edge
  His frozen medals spending.

Silent he lay, like Gulliver,
  Over the tiny town,
His heels kicking for cold at Brown Willy,
  His loins on Wilsey Down.

I saw his three-cornered hat
  Making an alp of the sky,
The snow flossing his blue coat and his buckles,
  Drifting his lip and his eye.

Brittle O brittle hangs the steeple:
  A finger of white,
The insidious snow furling, whirling
  In the glass ball of night.

Set forth so, imagination!
  Loot the locked turrets of light,
Speak with the tongues of bandits and angels,
  Put winter to flight!

AT PORTH VEOR

As I lay in my green ambush dreaming
  On the turreted cliff at Porth Veor
The sea pulling over the pebbles
  With long salt fingers below me,

There came on the west wind from Scilly
  The iron music of the London train
Carrying its cargo of freshly cut flowers
  To the porters and piazzas of Covent Garden.

And it seemed that again I walked the smoking city
  Among the baskets, the orange peel, the thieving boys.
Under the painted swinging signs at Temple Bar
  I walked to the sour Fleet.

It was a summer evening
  And fountaining on the clear air
I heard the music and the voices,
  I watched the frieze of swans upon the river.

And, briskly from a coach,
  A coach of wooden thunder,
There leapt a great bear of a man
  In a dirty brown wig and metal buttons.

None saw him in the crowded city save I:
  The Doctor, with his books and his oysters,
Striding up Bolt Court that summer evening.
  The old man, the swans, the thieving boys. . . .

As I lay in my green ambush dreaming
  On the turreted cliff at Porth Veor
The sea pulling over the pebbles
  With long salt fingers below me.

ABLE SEAMAN HODGE REMEMBERS CEYLON

O THE blackthorn and the wild cherry
  And the owl in the rotting oak tree
Are part of the Cornish landscape
  Which is more than can be said for me.

O the drum and the coconut fiddle
  And the taste of Arabian tea
The Vimto on the veranda
  And the arrack shops on the quay.

I wish I'd never heard of Kandy
  Or the song in the whiteflower tree.
(There's a thousand loafing matelots in the old
    base ship
  An' I wish that one of them was me.)

O the pineapple salads of Colombo
  The wine-bar at Trincomali
My bonnie lies over the ocean:
  The brilliant Arabian Sea.

arrack: alcohol made from coco-palm or rice

A VOYAGE FROM ITALY

To Barbara Cooper

The Italian ship 'Iota' was wrecked at Lye Beach near Tintagel in 1893. Two of the crew and a boy were drowned. The boy, Catanese Domenico, is buried in Tintagel churchyard.

HERE, Signora, slept my sea-boy
  Windowed by the flashing bay,
Where the sea-wall spread her sickle
  And the leaping fishboats lay.

On the bright sea's breast, my sea-boy,
  Curling to a different day;
The retreating lightship flashing
  Like a childhood, far away.

Sailing to the glittering river
  Or the fabled western strand,
As the pilfering sea forever
  Sidles on the crawling sand.

In his eye the shell-pink blossoms,
  On his tongue, the ilex tree;
His hair, the corn with yellow thunder,
  Holds the headland from the sea.

Never more he comes, Signora.
  The looping fountain silent stands.
He lies stiff in the bragging cliff,
  The blue sea-holly in his hands.

THE SEASONS IN NORTH CORNWALL

O SPRING has set off her green fuses
Down by the Tamar today,
And careless, like tide-marks, the hedges
Are bursting with almond and may.

Here lie I, waiting for old summer,
A red face and straw-coloured hair has he:
I shall meet him on the road from Marazion
And the Mediterranean Sea.

September has flung a spray of rooks
On the sea-chart of the sky,
The tall shipmasts crack in the forest
And the banners of autumn fly.

My room is a bright glass cabin,
All Cornwall thunders at my door,
And the white ships of winter lie
In the sea-roads of the moor.

RECRUITING DRIVE

UNDER the willow the willow
  I heard the butcher-bird sing,
Come out you fine young fellow
  From under your mother's wing.
I'll show you the magic garden
  That hangs in the beamy air,
The way of the lynx and the angry Sphinx
  And the fun of the freezing fair.

Lie down lie down with my daughter
  Beneath the Arabian tree,
Gaze on your face in the water
  Forget the scribbling sea.
Your pillow the nine bright shiners
  Your bed the spilling sand,
But the terrible toy of my lily-white boy
  Is the gun in his innocent hand.

You must take off your clothes for the doctor
  And stand as straight as a pin,
His hand of stone on your white breastbone
  Where the bullets all go in.
They'll dress you in lawn and linen
  And fill you with Plymouth gin,
O the devil may wear a rose in his hair
  I'll wear my fine doe-skin.

My mother weeps as I leave her
  But I tell her it won't be long,
The murderers wail in Wandsworth Gaol
  But I shoot a more popular song.
Down in the enemy country
  Under the enemy tree
There lies a lad whose heart has gone bad
  Waiting for me, for me.

He says I have no culture
  And that when I've stormed the pass
I shall fall on the farm with a smoking arm
  And ravish his bonny lass.
Under the willow the willow
  Death spreads her dripping wings
And caught in the snare of the bleeding air
  The butcher-bird sings, sings, sings.

PLYMOUTH

SOFT as the night and silent as the snow,
  Rain pours her arrows on the open city.
The sailor and his fancy homeward go
  And evening draws its shutter, as in pity.

Walking the sliding pavements, my feet
  Fiery as angels on the blazing stair,
I heard a strangling cornet in the street
  Volley its music on the falling air.

Blow, cornet, blow over the lurching channel
  Where the sleek sea for ever draws her comb!
A million matelots in the long sea-tunnel
  Hear your thin rumours, and remember home.

THE LIFE OF THE POET

LOCK the door, Schoolmaster,
Keep the children in.
The river in spate at the schoolyard gate
Roars like original sin.

Watch your thermometer, Sister,
The patient refuses to die.
The dizzy germ and the raving sperm
Can't keep his powder dry.

Strike the drum, Bandmaster,
Under the rig of the moon.
The girls come whirling, their veils unfurling,
But what has become of the tune?

Answer the door, Squire,
Your manners are on the table.
There's a job to be done with a humane gun
If the horse is still in the stable.

Draw your revolver, Banker,
Shoot him down like a dole.
You may gird his loins with nickel coins
But where's his immortal soul?

Open the book, Parson,
See whom you will save.
They say you're as kind as an open mind
Or an open grave.

Fall out, fall out, Gabriel,
You might as well hit the hay.
Your visitor wears the spinning airs
And won't be round today.

CORNWALL

ONE day, friend and stranger,
  The granite beast will rise
  Rubbing the salt sea from his hundred eyes
Sleeping no longer.

In the running river he will observe the tree
  Forging the slow signature of summer
  And like Caliban he will stumble and clamour
Crying *I am free! I am free!*

Night bares her silver wounds in the sky
  And flees from the shouting sun.
  O monster! What spear, what rock gun
Shall storm the fortress of your clear eyes?

Your teeth sharpened by many gliding waters,
  Lying awash in the snarling tide
  How long, how long must you wait to ride
Swagged with thunder on lovers and traitors?

Cast off your coloured stone ropes, signal the tourney!
  And to the bells of many drowned chapels
  Sail away, monster, leaving only ripples
Written in water to tell of your journey.

HOMAGE TO JACK CLEMO

IN THE deep wood dwells a demon
  Taller than any tree—
His prison bars are the sailing stars,
  His jailer is the sea.

With a brain and ten fingers
  He ties Cornwall to his table—
Imagination, at battle station,
  Guards Pegasus in his stable.

He walks the white hills of Egypt
  Reading the map of clay—
And through his night there moves the light
  Artillery of day.

Turn, Cornwall, turn and tear him!
  Stamp him in the sod!
He will not fear your cry so clear—
  Only the cry of God.

SONG OF THE WEATHER

WHEN the sun silts from the sky like an army descending
  To murder with light the silent city of spring,
When the wind vaults from its tall tower, defending
  The castle of snow from the touch of the eagle's wing,

When the river runs like a mad boy through the valley
  Seizing in strong sly fingers its sons and daughters,
When the sea leaps from sleep on the guiltless island
  And corrals it, fighting, in a noose of waters,

I think of my comrades locked in the map of Libya
  The desert flapping its heavy flag on their faces.
I see them wander deep in the blue forest
  Plucking the sea-orchid. I hear their voices

  Blown on the wind of summer, and the cry
  Of Icarus falling from the firing sky.

SERENADE TO A CORNISH FOX

As I sailed by the churchyard
  All on my wedding day
The bells in the seasick steeple
  Leaned over the side to say:

Hurry to harbour, sailor,
  Fetch the parson by noon
Or the fox will lie with your lover
  Under the mask of the moon.

Polish your ring, my captain,
  And crease your trousers well,
Take your crack at the tiller
  Or you'll crack your wedding bell.

But the sea is the matelot's mistress
  With her big blue baby eyes,
And many a master's ticket
  Has she torn in two for a prize.

Many a mariner's compass
  She has boxed with her watery hand,
As the fish jumped over the mountain
  And the ship sailed over the sand.

Over the waltzing water,
  Over the sober spray,
My ship sailed out of harbour
  All through the dancing day.

Down by the springy river,
  Down by the shrieking locks,
Watching love die, like a doctor
  Is the patient Mr Fox.

Down in the waving meadow
  Under the hanging tree
He is waiting as my lover
  Comes weeping in from sea.

See in her hand are flowers
  Of rosemary, and bay
Bright as the faithless water
  That took her love away.

Mr Fox, your topper is handy
  So put it over your ears.
Take the lace out of your pocket
  And dry her innocent tears.

Your coat is made of satin,
  Your wallet as gold as a harp,
The gloves on your delicate fingers
  Hide your nails so sharp.

O whisper the sea is randy
  And runs all over my head!
That she pulls me all so willing
  To her oozy marriage bed!

Farewell, my love my honey
  As my ship sails through the dark.
They have said the same of sailors
  Since Noah built the Ark.

May your daughters wear like diamonds
  Their virtue at their throats,
May your sons, like brave sea-bandits,
  Never take to the boats.

Only the fool or the poet
  Cuts down the flashing tree
To burn its belly with fire
  And take to the jealous sea.

RONDEL

GENERAL tell, when the red rose dying
  Snows with fire the watchful tree,
  As the blossoms burn do you turn to see
My body of stone on the bone beach lying?

General, spell when the wind sends sighing
  The sentence of light on the secret sea.
Do you crowd the loud lanes of water crying
  Drying your crocodile smile for me?

General, at your white head are flying
  The iron birds from the bolted tree.
  Gaze in the dawn on your lawn and see
The spies of night with your love are lying
Telling her you are dying, dying.

FAURÉ

TAKE me aboard your barque, where the valuable water
  Mirrors the perfect passage of the dove.
Over the glittering gulf the sun burns whiter
  The charts of envy and the reefs of love.

Lost in the frosty light the desperate hunter
  Hurls his black horn-note on the wrecked château
Where in despair the signalman of winter
  Winds on its walls the flashing flags of snow.

I see (captured my caravel) the stolen city
  Falling like Falcon to the cunning bay.
The holy sea, unmerciful and mighty,
  Strides with the tide its penance all the day.

Fling like a king your coin on the clear passage
  Bribing the sea-guard and the stumbling gun.
On the salt lawn scribble your last message
  Rallying the rout of ice on the storming sun.

ON THE THIRTEENTH DAY OF CHRISTMAS

ON THE thirteenth day of Christmas
  I saw King Jesus go
About the plain beyond my pane
  Wearing his cap of snow.

Sad was his brow as the snow-sky
  While all the world made merry,
In the black air his wounds burned bare
  As the fire in the holly berry.

At all the weeping windows
  The greedy children gather
And laugh at the clown in his white nightgown
  In the wicked winter weather.

I dragged the desperate city,
  I swagged the combing light,
I stood alone at the empty throne
  At the ninth hour of night.

On the thirteenth day of Christmas
  When the greasy guns bellow
His eye is dry as the splitting sky
  And his face is yellow.

I SAW A SHOT-DOWN ANGEL

I SAW a shot-down angel in the park
His marble blood sluicing the dyke of death,
A sailing tree firing its brown sea-mark
Where he now wintered for his wounded breath.

I heard the bird-noise of his splintered wings
Sawing the steep sierra of the sky,
On his fixed brow the jewel of the Kings
Reeked the red morning with a starving eye.

I stretched my hand to hold him from the heat,
I fetched a cloth to bind him where he bled,
I brought a bowl to wash his golden feet,
I shone my shield to save him from the dead.

My angel spat my solace in my face
And fired my fingers with his burning shawl,
Crawling in blood and silver to a place
Where he could turn his torture to the wall.

Alone I wandered in the sneaking snow
The signature of murder on my day,
And from the gallows-tree, a careful crow
Hitched its appalling wings and flew away.

OU PHRONTIS

To E. M. Forster

THE bells assault the maiden air,
The coachman waits with a carriage and pair,
But the bridegroom says *I won't be there,*
I don't care!

Three times three times the banns declare
That the boys may blush and the girls may glare,
But the bridegroom is occupied elsewhere,
I don't care!

Lord, but the neighbours all will stare,
Their temperatures jump as high as a hare,
But the bridegroom says *I've paid my fare,*
I don't care!

The bride she waits by the bed so bare,
Soft as a pillow is her hair,
But the bridegroom jigs with the leg of a chair,
I don't care!

Say, but her father's a millionaire,
A girdle of gold all night will she wear,
You must your foolish ways forswear.
I don't care!

Her mother will offer, if she dare,
A ring that is rich but not so rare
If you'll keep your friendship in repair.
I don't care!

Her sisters will give you a plum and a pear
And a diamond saddle for your mare.
O bridegroom! For the night prepare!
I don't care!

Her seven brothers all debonair
Will do your wishes and some to spare
If from your fancy you'll forbear.
I don't care!

Say, but a maid you wouldn't scare
Now that you've got her in your snare?
And what about your son and heir?
I don't care!

She'll leap, she'll leap from the highest stair,
She'll drown herself in the river there,
With a silver knife her flesh she'll tear.
I don't care!

Then another will lie in the silken lair
And cover with kisses her springing hair.
Another the bridal bed will share.
I don't care!

I shall stand on my head on the table bare,
I shall kick my lily-white legs in the air,
I shall wash my hands of the whole affair,
I don't care!

The words *Ou phrontis* were carved by T.E. Lawrence over the door of his cottage at Clouds Hill, Dorset. They come from the story in Herodotus on which this poem is based.

COWBOY SONG

I COME from Salem County
  Where the silver melons grow,
Where the wheat is sweet as an angel's feet
  And the zithering zephyrs blow.
I walk the blue bone-orchard
  In the apple-blossom snow,
When the teasy bees take their honeyed ease
  And the marmalade moon hangs low.

My Maw sleeps prone on the prairie
  In a boulder eiderdown,
Where the pickled stars in their little jam-jars
  Hang in a hoop to town.
I haven't seen Paw since a Sunday
  In eighteen seventy-three
When he packed his snap in a bitty mess-trap
  And said he'd be home by tea.

Fled is my fancy sister
  All weeping like the willow,
And dead is the brother I loved like no other
  Who once did share my pillow.
I fly the florid water
  Where run the seven geese round,
O the townsfolk talk to see me walk
  Six inches off the ground.

Across the map of midnight
  I trawl the turning sky,
In my green glass the salt fleets pass
  The moon her fire-float by.
The girls go gay in the valley
  When the boys come down from the farm,
Don't run, my joy, from a poor cowboy,
  I won't do you no harm.

The bread of my twentieth birthday
  I buttered with the sun,
Though I sharpen my eyes with lovers' lies
  I'll never see twenty-one.
Light is my shirt with lilies,
  And lined with lead my hood,
On my face as I pass is a plate of brass,
  And my suit is made of wood.

SAILOR'S CAROL

LORD, the snowful sky
  In this pale December
Fingers my clear eye
  Lest seeing, I remember

Not the naked baby
  Weeping in the stable
Nor the singing boys
  All round my table,

Not the dizzy star
  Bursting on the pane
Nor the leopard sun
  Pawing the rain.

Only the deep garden
  Where green lilies grow,
The sailors rolling
  In the sea's blue snow.

A GAME OF PATIENCE

In my garden the fly photographer
Assembles the gear of love,
His grinning page builds the sinning cage
Where beats the delicate dove.

Beneath the cool quilt of the filtering moon
The photographer bids me stay steady,
The bell-ringer stands with the rope in his hands,
But hangman, I am not ready.

On my winter walk I hear my friends talk
Of dogs and babies and gardens,
Blue on heaven's bar the acrobat star
Tumbles before the night hardens.

In the sour city I saw my true love,
Fine on her face the sweet rain,
In the street I will burn while the granite worlds
  turn
And carry her home again.

TO A POET WHO HAS NEVER TRAVELLED

As I rose like a lover from the ravished sea
My cold mouth stuffed with jewels and with sand,
The fire falling at my hair and hand,
(Her mother the moon waiting for the fee)
I saw you lying by the listening tree.

The infant pain lay sleeping at your side
Rocked by the naked fingers of the tide,
But you saw not my shaking ship, nor me.

I spread my sweating sea-charts at your knee
My rooted tongue burgeoning apes and roses
As noon the sally-port of morning closes,
My crew hallooing at the drunken quay.

My bonny barque was sundered at your door!
You smiled, for you had seen it all before.

sally-port: opening for making sallies from a fortified place

ON SEEING A POET OF THE FIRST WORLD WAR ON THE STATION AT ABBEVILLE

POET, cast your careful eye
Where the beached songs of summer lie,
  White fell the wave that splintered
  The wreck where once you wintered,
White as the snows that lair
Your freezing hair.

Captain, here you took your wine,
The trees at ease in the orchard-line,
  Bonny the errand-boy bird
  Whistles the songs you once heard,
While you traverse the wire,
Autumn will hold her fire.

Through the tall wood the thunder ran
As when the gibbering guns began,
  Swift as a murderer by the stack
  Crawled the canal with fingers black,
Black with your brilliant blood
You lit the mud.

Two grey moths stare from your eyes,
Sharp is your sad face with surprise.
  In the stirring pool I fail
  To see the drowned of Passchendaele,
Where all day drives for me
The spoiling sea.

BALLAD OF THE FAITHLESS WIFE

CARRY her down to the river
  Carry her down to the sea
Let the bully-boys stare at her braided hair
  But never a glance from me.

Down by the writhing water
  Down by the innocent sand
They laid my bride by the toiling tide
  A stone in her rifled hand.

Under the dainty eagle
  Under the ravening dove
Under a high and healthy sky
  I waited for my love.

Off she ran with a soldier
  Tall as a summer tree,
Soft as a mouse he came to my house
  And stole my love from me.

O splintered were all the windows
  And broken all the chairs
War like a knife ran through my life
  And the blood ran down the stairs.

Loud on the singing morning
  I hear the mad birds rise
Safe from harm to the sun's alarm
  As the sound of fighting dies.

I would hang my harp on the branches
  And weep all through the day
But stranger, see! The wounded tree
  Has burned itself away.

False O false was my lover
  Dead on the diamond shore
White as a fleece, for her name was Peace
  And the soldier's name was War.

SHORE LEAVE

SEE the moon her yellow landau
Draws across the fainting sky.
The white owl round my window wanders
As I hurry by.

Night the Negro lays his fingers
On the lily-breast of day.
Sleep beckons like a gentle lover
But I hasten away.

On the sea the ships are leaping
To the islands of the sun.
On the deck the sailors sleeping
Would I were one!

In my ear no more the music
Of the tree the summer long,
Only the unfaithful ocean
And the Sirens' song.

I AM THE GREAT SUN

From a Normandy crucifix of 1632

I AM the great sun, but you do not see me,
  I am your husband, but you turn away.
I am the captive, but you do not free me,
  I am the captain you will not obey.

I am the truth, but you will not believe me,
  I am the city where you will not stay,
I am your wife, your child, but you will leave me,
  I am that God to whom you will not pray.

I am your counsel, but you do not hear me,
  I am the lover whom you will betray,
I am the victor, but you do not cheer me,
  I am the holy dove whom you will slay.

I am your life, but if you will not name me,
Seal up your soul with tears, and never blame me.

AT THE STATUE OF WILLIAM THE CONQUEROR, FALAISE

SEE him ride the roaring air
In an iron moustache and emerald hair,
Furious with flowers on a foundry cob
The bastard son of the late Lord Bob.

He writes his name with a five-flagged spear
On skies of infantry in the rear
And fixed at his feet, in chainmail stations,
Six unshaven Norman relations:

Rollo, Guillaume Longue-Épée,
Le Bon, Sans Peur, Richard Three,
Robert the Devil; and over them all
The horse's tail, like a waterfall.

Many a shell struck Talbot's Tower
From Henry the Fifth to Eisenhower,
But never a splinter scratched the heel
Of the bully in bronze at the Hôtel de Ville.

On the chocolate wall of the tall château
Tansy, pimpernel, strawberry grow;
And down by the tanyard the washing hangs wet
As it did in the dirty days of Arlette.

Hubert and Arthur and Holy Joan
Knew this staring stack of stone
Where William scowls in a Saracen cap
And sat out the fight for the famous Gap.

Gallop on, General with cider eyes,
Until the snow-coasts of Sussex rise!
Silence the tearful and smiling with thunder
As you spring from the sea, bringing history under.

AT THE BRITISH WAR CEMETERY, BAYEUX

I WALKED where in their talking graves
And shirts of earth five thousand lay,
When history with ten feasts of fire
Had eaten the red air away.

'I am Christ's boy,' I cried. 'I bear
In iron hands the bread, the fishes.
I hang with honey and with rose
This tidy wreck of all your wishes.

'On your geometry of sleep
The chestnut and the fir-tree fly,
And lavender and marguerite
Forge with their flowers an English sky.

'Turn now towards the belling town
Your jigsaws of impossible bone,
And rising read your rank of snow
Accurate as death upon the stone.'

About your easy heads my prayers
I said with syllables of clay.
'What gift,' I asked, 'shall I bring now
Before I weep and walk away?'

Take, they replied, *the oak and laurel.*
Take our fortune of tears and live
Like a spendthrift lover. All we ask
Is the one gift you cannot give.

A TRUE BALLAD OF SIR HENRY TRECARELL

who in 1511 rebuilt the parish church of St Mary Magdalene at Launceston in Cornwall

HENRY TRECARELL sat up in bed
His face was white and his eyes were red,
'I dreamed,' he cried, 'that our son was dead!'
'Lie over, Sir Henry,' her ladyship said.

'I saw him sink in a silver fen
In the arms of a wicked white Magdalene.
I hope I'm imagining things!' Only then
Her ladyship murmured, 'Amen! Amen!

'The moon walks west on the orchard wall,
Your daughters are dozing over the Hall
And your son sleeps as sound as a cannon-ball.
There is nothing the matter, Sir Henry, at all!'

But when the boy-baby, as naked as sin,
Stood up in a cold Cornish basin of tin
His nurse went away for a little napkin
And he fell on the water and breathed it all in.

The carpenters no longer whistled a carol.
Said Margaret to Henry (in mourning apparel):
'You'll finish the Manor, with roof like a barrel?'
'I'm damned if I will,' said Sir Henry Trecarell.

Sir Henry's and Margaret's tears fell hard
And their two Tudor faces were sorry as lard
As they built in the baby beneath the churchyard
In a parcel of linen and spikenard.

When Sir Henry descended one evening to dine
The Magdalene told him to build her a shrine,
But her ladyship said, as she poured out the wine,
'I'd hoped you'd forgotten that concubine.'

Sir Henry Trecarell stood at his ewer
And gazed at the granite among the manure.
He called out, 'My grief I'll no longer endure!
Send for the Mayor—John Bonaventure.'

The limbers all lugged the stone in from Lezant
And the running-boys heard sad Sir Henry chant:
'To the Glory of God this stone tree I now plant
For Mary, and Henry the Protestant.'

For twelve years and one in Launceston town
The masons wore fifty flint fingers down
Carving an angel, a rose or a clown
On every inch of the Magdalene's crown.

While Flodden was fought and the Frenchmen fell
  low
And Cortés was conquering Mexico,
When Wolsey was Generalissimo
They hammered away at the holy château.

When the sun in the summer is spreading his hood
The beggar still sulks in the starving mud,
The pelican glides with a gift of blood
And the eagle ascends to the throne of good.

Where winter descends with her smudging snow
The nardus and pomegranate grow,
And through the forest the frozen doe,
The greyhound, the griffin and honey-bear go.

nardus: the spikenard plant

The immortal yew and the frigid oak
Stand about Martin slicing his cloak,
And George (on a pony) tries to invoke
The dragon, making crystal smoke.

Now the Magdalene lies on a mica strand
Spreading her hair with an idle hand,
And ready to play at her command
Is a sawing sixteenth-century band.

The ointment stands at the Magdalene's side,
St Matthew's Gospel is open wide,
And round the wall the writings ride:
Behold! The Bridegroom loves the Bride!

Sir Henry Trecarell went up to bed
The pains all gone from his heart and head.
'My life,' he cried, 'is newly wed!'
'Praised be the Lord,' her ladyship said.

THE POET'S FAREWELL TO HIS MUSE

GOODBYE Tom Pretty
I'm off to the city
Its yellow lights leering.
Soft as spring weather
My breeches of leather
And the silk shirt I'm wearing.

Tom Pretty, peruse
In the mirror of shoes
My honey-bright parting.
Sparkling my mare
Strikes the stone stair,
I must be starting.

My doxy she sighs
And wet are her eyes
But the weeping sea's wetter,
And Tom Pretty, soon
The corruptible moon
Says I'll go one better.

When winter came down
On the terrible town
And beat his black sabre,
I rode in the rain
His prison of pain
And found no neighbour.

Tom Pretty, your head
From your true love's bed
Turn at my calling.
The Furies ride
At my speared side
And the snow is falling.

HYMN FOR THE BIRTH OF A ROYAL PRINCE

PRINCE, for your throat of ice
The tigers of the sun
Rehearse with quarrels of fire
Their chosen one.

Upon your breast of lambs
The lean assassin lies
With love upon his lips
And chaos in his eyes.

About your brittle bed
The seven sharp angels stay
That from the frigid knife
You know will turn away.

The bawling organ breaks
Upon the appalling stone
Whose quiet courtier takes
Your kingdom for his own.

The warriors drub their wands,
With pearl your footsteps pave,
But dribbles at your feet
The idiot grave.

Prince, to your throne of birds
May all my passions fly
That, guilty, I may live
And you may die!

TIMOTHY WINTERS

TIMOTHY WINTERS comes to school
With eyes as wide as a football pool,
Ears like bombs and teeth like splinters:
A blitz of a boy is Timothy Winters.

His belly is white, his neck is dark,
And his hair is an exclamation mark.
His clothes are enough to scare a crow
And through his britches the blue winds blow.

When teacher talks he won't hear a word
And he shoots down dead the arithmetic-bird,
He licks the patterns off his plate
And he's not even heard of the Welfare State.

Timothy Winters has bloody feet
And he lives in a house on Suez Street,
He sleeps in a sack on the kitchen floor
And they say there aren't boys like him any more.

Old Man Winters likes his beer
And his missus ran off with a bombardier,
Grandma sits in the grate with a gin
And Timothy's dosed with an aspirin.

The Welfare Worker lies awake
But the law's as tricky as a ten-foot snake,
So Timothy Winters drinks his cup
And slowly goes on growing up.

At Morning Prayers the Master helves
For children less fortunate than ourselves,
And the loudest response in the room is when
Timothy Winters roars 'Amen!'

helves: a dialect word from north Cornwall used to describe the alarmed lowing of cattle (as when a cow is separated from her calf); a desperate, pleading note

So come one angel, come on ten:
Timothy Winters says 'Amen
Amen amen amen amen.'
Timothy Winters, Lord.
                    Amen.

HAWTHORN WHITE

HAWTHORN white, hawthorn red
Hanging in the garden at my head
Tell me simple, tell me true
When comes the winter what must I do?

I have a house with chimneys four
I have a silver bell on the door,
A single hearth and a single bed.
  Not enough, the hawthorn said.

I have a lute, I have a lyre
I have a yellow cat by my fire,
A nightingale to my tree is tied.
  That bird looks sick, the hawthorn sighed.

I write on paper pure as milk
I lie on sheets of shantung silk,
On my green breast no sin has snowed.
  You'll catch your death, the hawthorn crowed.

My purse is packed with a five-pound note
The watchdogs in my garden gloat.
I blow the bagpipe down my side.
  Better blow your safe, the hawthorn cried.

My pulse is steady as my clock
My wits are wise as the weathercock.
Twice a year we are overhauled.
  It's Double Summer Time! the hawthorn called.

I have a horse with wings for feet
I have chicken each day to eat.
When I was born the church-bells rang.
  Only one at a time, the hawthorn sang.

I have a cellar, I have a spread
The bronze blood runs round my bulkhead:
Why is my heart as light as lead?
  Love is not there, the hawthorn said.

DEATH OF AN AIRCRAFT

To George Psychoundakis

An incident of the Cretan campaign, 1941

ONE day on our village in the month of July
An aeroplane sank from the sea of the sky,
  White as a whale it smashed on the shore
  Bleeding oil and petrol all over the floor.

The Germans advanced in the vertical heat
To save the dead plane from the people of Crete,
  And round the glass wreck in a circus of snow
  Set seven mechanical sentries to go.

Seven stalking spiders about the sharp sun
Clicking like clockwork and each with a gun,
  But at 'Come to the cookhouse' they wheeled
    about
  And sat down to sausages and *sauerkraut*.

Down from the mountain burning so brown
Wriggled three heroes from Kastelo town,
  Deep in the sand they silently sank
  And each struck a match for a petrol tank.

Up went the plane in a feather of fire
As the bubbling boys began to retire
  And, grey in the guardhouse, seven Berliners
  Lost their stripes as well as their dinners.

Down in the village, at murder-stations,
The Germans fell in friends and relations:
  But not a Kastelian snapped an eye
  As he spat in the air and prepared to die.

Not a Kastelian whispered a word
Dressed with the dust to be massacred,
  And squinted up at the sky with a frown
  As three bubbly boys came walking down.

One was sent to the county gaol
Too young for bullets if not for bail,
  But the other two were in prime condition
  To take on a load of ammunition.

In Archontiki they stood in the weather
Naked, hungry, chained together:
  Stark as the stones in the market place,
  Under the eyes of the populace.

Their irons unlocked as their naked hearts
They faced the squad and their funeral-carts.
  The Captain cried, 'Before you're away
  Is there any last word you'd like to say?'

'I want no words,' said one, 'with my lead,
Only some water to cool my head.'
  'Water,' the other said, ''s all very fine
  But I'll be taking a glass of wine.

'A glass of wine for the afternoon
With permission to sing a signature tune!'
  And he ran the *raki* down his throat
  And took a deep breath for the leading note.

But before the squad could shoot or say
Like the impala he leapt away
  Over the rifles, under the biers,
  The bullets rattling round his ears.

'Run!' they cried to the boy of stone
Who now stood there in the street alone,
  But, 'Rather than bring revenge on your head
  It is better for me to die,' he said.

The soldiers turned their machine-guns round
And shot him down with a dreadful sound
  Scrubbed his face with perpetual dark
  And rubbed it out like a pencil mark.

But his comrade slept in the olive tree
And sailed by night on the gnawing sea,
  The soldier's silver shilling earned
  And, armed like an archangel, returned.

THE PRISONERS OF LOVE

TRAPPED in their tower, the prisoners of love
Loose their last message on the failing air.
The troops of Tyre assault with fire the grove
Where Venus veils with light her lovely hair.

Trembles the tide beneath the tall martello
That decks the harbour with its wreck of thunder,
Fretting with flowers white and flowers yellow
The fosse of flame into its last surrender.

Night, on my truckle-bed your ease of slumber
Sleep in salt arms the steering night away.
Abandoned in the fireship moon, one ember
Glows with the rose that is the distant day.

The prisoners rise and rinse their skies of stone,
But in their jailers' eyes they meet their own.

MEVAGISSEY

PETER jumped up in the pulpit
His hands all smelling of fish,
His guernsey was gay with the sparky spray
And white as an angel's wish.

The seagulls came in through the ceiling
The fish flew up through the floor,
Bartholomew laughed as he cast off aft
And Andrew cast off fore.

They charged the thundering churchyard
Like a lifeboat down the slip,
And the congregation in consternation
Prepared to abandon ship.

Overboard went the bonnets
Over went the bowlers
And, before the seas were up to their knees,
A hundred holy rollers.

'Draw your tots!' said Peter,
'Every man to his post!
It's not so far to heaven's bar
With the charts I've got of the coast!

'Shoot the boom like Satan!
Prepare to take on boarders!
Send up your prayers like signal-flares!
I'll steam the secret orders!

'Stoke up the engine-room boilers
With slices of heavenly toast!
The devil's a weasel and travels on diesel
But I burn the Holy Ghost!'

What became of the vessel
Nobody dared inquire,
But the new church-room is tough as a tomb
And the walls are very much higher.

Its anchor is glittering granite,
Its cable is long as Lent,
But the winds won't reek, and refuse to speak
In a silent sail of cement.

Its mast is made of iron,
Its gunwales are made of lead,
Its cargo of bone is hard as the stone
That hangs about my head.

I walk all day in the dockyard
Looking for Captain Pete,
But there's not a marine or a brigantine
At the bottom of Harbour Street.

The boy-voiced boat, like summer,
Has sailed away over the hills
And I'm beached like a bride by the travelling tide
With a packet of seasick pills.

BETJEMAN, 1984

I SAW him in the Airstrip Gardens
  (Fahrenheit at 451)
Feeding automative orchids
  With a little plastic bun,
While above his brickwork cranium
  Burned the trapped and troubled sun.

'Where is Piper? Where is Pontefract?
  (Devil take my boiling pate!)
Where is Pam? And where's Myfanwy?
  Don't remind me of the date!
Can it be that I am *really*
  Knocking on for seventy-eight?

'In my splendid State Apartment
  Underneath a secret lock
Finger now forbidden treasures
  (Pray for me St Enodoc!):
TV plate and concrete lamp-post
  And a single nylon sock.

'Take your ease, pale-haired admirer,
  As I, half the century saner,
Pour a vintage Mazawattee
  Through the Marks & Spencer strainer
In a *genuine* British Railways
  (Luton Made) cardboard container.

'Though they say my verse-compulsion
  Lacks an interstellar drive,
Reading Beverley and Daphne
  Keeps *my* sense of words alive.
Lord, but *how* much beauty was there
  Back in 1955!'

ARMISTICE DAY

I STOOD with three comrades in Parliament Square
November her freights of grey fire unloading,
No sound from the city upon the pale air,
Above us the sea-bell eleven exploding.

Down by the bands and the burning memorial
Beats all the brass in a royal array,
But at our end we are not so sartorial:
Out of (as usual) the rig of the day.

Starry is wearing a split pusser's flannel
Rubbed, as he is, by the regular tide;
Oxo the ducks that he ditched in the Channel
In June, 1940 (when he was inside).

Kitty recalls his abandon-ship station,
Running below at the Old Man's salute
And (with a deck-watch) going down for duration
Wearing his oppo's pneumonia-suit.

Comrades, for you the black captain of carracks
Writes in Whitehall his appalling decisions,
But as was often the case in the Barracks
Several ratings are not at Divisions.

Into my eyes the stiff sea-horses stare,
Over my head sweeps the sun like a swan.
As I stand alone in Parliament Square
A cold bugle calls, and the city moves on.

pusser's flannel: naval-issue shirt
ducks: white duck-suit
oppo: from 'opposite number'; friend; comrade
pneumonia-suit: tropical rig; or canvas suit worn while painting ship, etc.

COLONIAL SONG

LOVE me early, love me late
Love me down by the Charles Five Gate
Love me fierce as a nuclear fission
Say you'll stay on a long commission.
Meek on the Mediterranean air
When Bandie blows 'Shore leave' I'll be there.

Love me fast, love me slow
Tell me all I want to know
As you dance on a dicky-run ashore
Bring every pearl from the pusser's store.
Under my table the legs are wide:
All your ship's company is sitting inside.

Hang your kisses about my throat
I'll burn a hole in your lammy-coat
Let the dead marines lie where they are
We'll play a tune on the bumble-jar,
And after supper you shall chart
The canteen medals round my heart.

O what is it now, you swine, you suggest?
Take your grabhooks off my Persil breast!
Take your ticklers! Take your grease!
Send for my brother in the Dockyard Police!
Take your gippo and take your jam!
What kind of a girl do you think I am?

dicky: quick
'All your ship's company is sitting inside': café tout's cry
lammy: fireproof
dead marines: empties
bumble-jar: gramophone
canteen medals: food stains
grabhooks: fingers
ticklers: cigarettes made from duty-free tobacco
grease: butter
gippo: gravy

Stop the fire main! Dry off the hose!
Haul down the garland that on the mast grows
Put him in the rattle! Send him to the brig!
All you'll get from me is a Saltash rig.
Finished with the duty watch; replace gear.
Send for the Jaunty *and get him out of here!*

garland: i.e. for a wedding
in the rattle: on a charge
Saltash rig: wetting and nothing to show for it
Jaunty: Master-at-Arms

TIME LIKE A SAUCY TROOPER

TIME like a saucy trooper took my true love
In the stiff corn that stands above the bay.
Never a backward glance he gave his new love,
But whistled a tune and slowly rode away.

About her brow my love winds the white hours
And binds her breast with sprigs of rosemary.
Through her thin hands she threads the winter flowers
And lies with eyes as pale as the snowy sea.

Ruined the roses on the giddy river
That heaps its tears upon the sleeping narrows.
The archer sun unships his candid quiver
And tips with azure all his blazing arrows.

Now the swift seasons, coasting shores of sorrow,
On the wild waters sink their chinking floes,
And for the tender promise of tomorrow
They leave the lily, but uproot the rose.

I made my love a hive of yellow honey,
I laid my love a cabin on the water,
Two beds I bought of my new-minted money
For my true love and me, and for her daughter.

Never across the water comes she winging,
Bright is our bed as on its boughten day,
And all the night I hear my lover singing
The song the soldier sang as he rode away.

AT THE RUIN OF BODMIN GAOL

I UNLOCKED a box that once was sprung with clay
Its crazy birds through cruel hatches flying,
With hands of storms I hurled its roof away
And furled with bandaged sky the quick, the dying.

In the steel château a thousand soldiers sleeping,
Swearing, despairing on their shattered suns,
Saw the stone days, their seven dolours keeping,
Strangle with rose and bay the signal-guns.

I heard the heart's drum in the scratched cell beating
Where men had danced like rams that love was slain,
The whirling birds in staves of trees repeating
Within the walls their arabesques of pain.

About the bitter air their songs they strung
And as they shot with shivering darts my tongue
I saw my Son, naked as Eden, turning
And on his head a bough of thorns was burning.

BALLAD OF THE FIVE CONTINENTS

IN BLUE Bristol city at tall-tide I wandered
  Down where the sea-masts their signals were shining,
  I heard a proud seaman on the poop deck reclining
Shout to the stars that about the ship blundered
  'On the high harbour lie six shifty daughters
  Their bodies are straight, their eyes are wide
  Here is the key of their burly bedchamber'
I have unlocked it, I replied.

As I went down Water Street beneath the blond sun
  The trees of cold Christmas screaming with starlings
  Sweet screamed the birds as my delicate darlings
Scanned at my hand the black-buttered gun
  'Think of the collar my bonny, my beauty
  Think of the hangman with hands so red
  Pray, pray that he does his duty'
I am that hangman, I said.

As I walked in Wine Street the silk snow was falling
  And night in her Asian hair hung her comb,
  Soft sang the yellow-faced seaman of home
The gong and the coconut-fiddle recalling
  'In the vermilion forest the dancer
  Adorns with gold thorns his holy head
  Will you not seize his hands, his fingers?'
I am the dance, I said.

In Bread Street in summer we saw the boys hauling
  The Yankee-white wheat on the bowl of the bay,
  Between us the sword of the sun where we lay
Bloody with poppies, the warm sky our shawling
  'Sly sing the sirens on the coast of California
  The oyster-fingered, the easy-eyed,
  Tiding their tune in the gin-wicked palaces'
The song is mine, I cried.

Down by the dockside the green ships groaning
  Ten-roped writhe on the ragged sea,
  Blessed are they with the laurel tree
Now in the prow stands a saint for the stoning
  'Sound the salt bell on the mound of the ocean
  Fish for a prayer in the pool of the dead
  When the storm strikes, speak the word on the waters'
I am that word, I said.

ENVOI

I am the Prince
I am the lowly
I am the damned
I am the holy.
My hands are ten knives.
I am the dove
Whose wings are murder.
My name is love.

INNOCENT'S SONG

WHO'S that knocking on the window,
Who's that standing at the door,
What are all those presents
Lying on the kitchen floor?

Who is the smiling stranger
With hair as white as gin,
What is he doing with the children
And who could have let him in?

Why has he rubies on his fingers,
A cold, cold crown on his head,
Why, when he caws his carol,
Does the salty snow run red?

Why does he ferry my fireside
As a spider on a thread,
His fingers made of fuses
And his tongue of gingerbread?

Why does the world before him
Melt in a million suns,
Why do his yellow, yearning eyes
Burn like saffron buns?

Watch where he comes walking
Out of the Christmas flame,
Dancing, double-talking:

Herod is his name.

PRINZ EUGEN

PRINZ EUGEN walked on the castle wall,
His eye was long and his leg was tall.
'Do you not fear, Prince,' I said, 'you will fall?'
Never, he answered. *Never at all.*

'Gold is your head and gold your groin,
Your nose is as neat as a Roman coin.
The spin of your skin has never a join!'

Look, said the Prince, *at my lip and my loin.*
Look at the silver that springs from my thumb,
Look for the brown blood that never will come.
Teach my beached heart the soft speech of the drum,
Feather with words the straw birds as they hum.
On my cold castle the strict sea knocks,
Butters his blade on the rim of the rocks.
Do you not hear how his ticking tongue mocks,
Slits every second and keel-hauls the clocks?

'Prince, but your gilt-edged eyebrow curls,
You stop your sentences up with pearls.
What will you do with all the girls
When love his lamp-black flag unfurls?
And Prince, your platinum fingers play
Over the maps and far away.
Are you not lord of all you survey?'
Then I am blind, I heard him say.

'Bright is your bed as the sailing shore,
Its posters up to the ceiling soar.
The servants stand at your dazzling door
To strip your senses to the core.
White is the light at your driven head,
Your body of corn stands straight as bread.
Why is your beating breast unfed?
Is it because you are dead, are dead?'

Envy me not this cloth of clay
That dries to dust all through the day.
Hurtle your heart on the pouring bay,
Answered Prinz Eugen, and limped away.

MOTHER, GET UP, UNBAR THE DOOR

MOTHER, get up, unbar the door,
Throw wide the window-pane,
I see a man stand all covered in sand
Outside in Vicarage Lane.

His body is shot with seventy stars,
His face is cold as Cain,
His coat is a crust of desert dust
And he comes from Alamein.

He has not felt the flaking frost,
He has not felt the rain,
And not one blow of the burning snow
Since the night that he was slain.

O mother, in your husband's arms
Too long now you have lain,
Rise up, my dear, your true love's here
Upon the peaceful plain.

Though, mother, on your broken brow
Forty long years are lain,
The soldier they slew at twenty-two
Never a one does gain.

I will unlock the fine front door
And snap the silver chain,
And meek as milk in my skin of silk
I'll ease him of his pain.

My breast has been for years eighteen
As white as Charles's Wain,
But now I'm had by a soldier lad
Whistling 'Lili Marlene'.

Farewell to Jack, farewell to Jim,
And farewell Mary Jane,
Farewell the good green sisterhood
Knitting at purl and plain.

Go wash the water from your eye,
The bullet from your brain.
I'm drowned as a dove in the tunnel of love
And I'll never come home again.

EMBLEMS OF THE PASSION

Here, you said, the voice well-bred
Carried in that classic head,
Unremarking, as your fashion,
That the slipping sky was ashen,
Are the Emblems of the Passion.

Overhead a heeling bird
Struck on the split sky the word,
But I do not think you heard
As the blood of the last sun
On the wounded water spun.

Safe beneath a shooting spire
Here you waded the green wire
Of the graveyard's fallen fire,
Dreams, desires, as fish asleep
In the silence of its deep.

On the raging wood, unread
Histories of the hanged, the dead
Searched the cyphers of my head:
Soldier, seamless robe on rail,
Hyssop, hammer, crown and nail.

From the forest of my fears
Thirty-coined, a tree of tears
Flowered on the sour, slab floor
By the high, the holy door
Of death's strict and silent shore.

Hand with scourges, hand with spear,
Lantern, ladder, cross and gear,
Cock on pillar. Chaste and clear
God's trapping tongue: *Consider this*
Head of Judas, and the kiss.

Underneath that seamless sky
Stripped, I met your startled eye
Saw your sweating lip, and I
Whose face was Judas, felt you start
At the rivers of the heart.

CRISTO DE BRISTOL

The 'Cristo de Bristol' is an articulated figure of Christ used for the Easter Sepulchre and carried through the streets of a fishing village of northern Spain during the Holy Week processions. It is said to have been dredged from the Avon by a Spanish sea-captain, who brought the figure to his home port.

I AM the Bristol Christ,
That waking man who won
With hands of wire the Easter fire
Out of the Biscay sun.
Cast in my coat of lights
Upon the poking tide
A seaman with a snare of stars
Hauled me to his side.

Swim on, Captain Jesus,
Wherever you may wish.
Write on the wicked water
The message of the fish.
Heal in the holy river
Your five and fingered scars,
Turn like a tree about the sea
Your skeleton of spars.

I stepped from off the ocean
Upon the sea-struck shore,
I laid me down my cruel crown
Before my father's door.
I carried him that kingdom
I set beneath my skin
That he might seal the sorrow
Of all the world within.

Now springs upon your shipmast
The burning bush of day,
From your shot side the breathing tide
Wears the black grave away.
Bless with your fan of fingers
These hands, this heart, these eyes,
And lift my love and fishes
Perfect, to Paradise.

O BILLY, DO YOU HEAR THAT BELL?

O BILLY, do you hear that bell
  Speaking from the spire?
Has Willie Fell gone down the well
  Or is it *Fire, fire*?
And do you see a cinder star
  Sizzling in the sky,
And crazy Kings with burning wings
  Learning how to fly?

O sister, soft as any shawl
  The sharp snow winds the wire,
Pale as a pall the cattle trawl
  Their breath about the byre.
Now in the rare and eating air
  The bird chinks on the thorn,
And slowly through the holy blue
  The shepherd hauls his horn.

O father, is that cruel cry
  Coming from the mire
A Wise Man lost in the world's frost
  Or is it only Squire?
And when the alleluia boys
  Drum their December din,
Why do you call the constable
  That he may lock them in?

O mother, who will find the flock
  And harness up the shire,
And who will lock the weather-clock
  If winter does not tire,
And who will ship a farthing dip
  Upon the drifting day,
And seize a spark from heaven's dark
  To burn the night away?

O Billy, will you wag the word
  From off your freezing tongue,
Nor hire the hearse or district nurse
  Because I am so young?
And shall we push the business on
  And do the best we can
To cut free from the Christmas tree
  The hanging, holy man?

SONNET TO THE HOLY VINE

On the report of an oppressed Spanish donkey who, after drinking eighteen pints of wine, turned on his persecutors and won a new independence.

HERE sleeps Don Diego, *burro*, of this city,
The sticks of Jesus strapped upon his spine,
Who burned away his pack of pain and pity
In fires of garnet gathered from the vine.
Through the white winter and the summer shine
He laboured for the kingdom of the ape
Until he wrote his talking throat with wine
And grasped eternity within the grape.
Before Don Diego, Phoebus-tongued with flares,
Doctor, priest, lawyer, soldier of the line,
Rose from their knees and with a hundred prayers
They bore his skin of battle to this shrine
Where he now lies beneath the throbbing thorn
And in three days will rise, like man, reborn.

MASTER AND PUPIL

On a theme of Demetrios Capetanakis

HE SHOOK the bandage from his snowing head,
Flooded with fire his hollow heart of stone.
It was as clear as blood, the neighbours said.
The old man had no children of his own.

When they both walked upon the sharp sea-shore,
He with his hand within the gold boy's breast,
The colours of the cock the winter wore
And the sun faltered in the flowing west.

We never can forget that sight, they cried.
Who would have thought of murder, the police?
It was as if, somehow, we all had spied
Some mentionable scene from Ancient Greece.

A Sunday paper printed all the facts,
Developing in paschal blood their day.
There was a front-page picture of the axe,
But all the innocence was wiped away.

No greater love has any man than this
That lays a friend's life down to save his own,
They murmur, sealing with a loving kiss
The cracked, cold body in its suit of stone.

He never spilt an atom of regret,
They sigh. *The boy shows no respect for death,*
As on the striking day he hangs his debt,
Stands on the hour and sucks a last, strapped breath.

AT GRANTCHESTER

BANK Holiday. A sky of guns. The river
Slopping black silver on the level stair.
A war memorial that aims for ever
Its stopped, stone barrel on the enormous air.

A hoisted church, its cone of silence stilling
The conversations of the crow, the kite.
A coasting chimney-stack, advancing, filling
With smoking blossom the lean orchard light.

The verse, I am assured, has long ceased ticking
Though the immortal clock strikes ten to three.
The fencing wasp fights for its usual picking
And tongues of honey hang from every tree.

The swilling sea with its unvarying thunder
Explores the secret face of famous stone.
On the thrown wind blown words like hurt birds wander
That from the maimed, the murdered mouth have flown.

HEALING A LUNATIC BOY

TREES turned and talked to me,
  Tigers sang,
Houses put on leaves,
  Water rang.
Flew in, flew out
  On my tongue's thread
A speech of birds
  From my hurt head.

At my fine loin
  Fire and cloud kissed,
Rummaged the green bone
  Beneath my wrist.
I saw a sentence
  Of fern and tare
Write with loud light
  The mineral air.

On a stopped morning
  The city spoke,
In my rich mouth
  Oceans broke.
No more on the spun shore
  I walked unfed.
I drank the sweet sea,
  Stones were bread.

Then came the healer
  Grave as grass,
His hair of water
  And hands of glass.
I watched at his tongue
  The white words eat,
In death, dismounted
  At his stabbed feet.

Now river is river
  And tree is tree,
My house stands still
  As the northern sea.
On my hundred of parables
  I heard him pray,
Seize my smashed world,
  Wrap it away.

Now the pebble is sour,
  The birds beat high,
The fern is silent,
  The river dry.
A seething summer
  Burned to bone
Feeds at my mouth
  But finds a stone.

MISS ELLIOTT

LITTLE Miss Elliott died in the dark
At 95 Victoria Park.

I saw as I strolled in the ivory air
The Prince of Darkness stand on her stair,

Scaled in sharp black from cap to toe,
About him his soldiers swarming like snow,

Armed with all hell and bladed with light,
Banners and torches and thunderbolts bright,

War-horses hammering holes in the sky,
Waiting for little Miss Elliott to die.

And as Miss Elliott her final breath furled
Out of the vertical midnight they hurled,

Drawing their swords from the corpse of the sun,
A million warriors falling on one.

But, as they slung down the shattering air,
Little Miss Elliott was no longer there:

I saw, as they sank with the sound of the swan,
Little Miss Elliott had gone, gone, gone.

FOR AN EX-FAR EAST PRISONER OF WAR

I AM that man with helmet made of thorn
Who wandered naked in the desert place,
Wept, with the sweating sky, that I was born
And wore disaster in my winter face.

I am that man who asked no hate, nor pity.
I am that man, five-wounded, on the tree.
I am that man, walking his native city,
Hears his dead comrade cry, *Remember me!*

I am that man whose brow with blood was wet,
Returned, as Lazarus, from the dead to live.
I am that man, long counselled to forget,
Facing a fearful victory, to forgive:

And seizing these two words, with the sharp sun
Beat them, like sword and ploughshare, into one.

MY FRIEND MALONEY

MY FRIEND Maloney, eighteen,
  Swears like a sentry,
Got into trouble two years back
  With the local gentry.

Parson and squire's sons
  Informed a copper.
The magistrate took one look at Maloney.
  Fixed him proper.

Talked of the crime of youth,
  The innocent victim.
Maloney never said a blind word
  To contradict him.

Maloney of Gun Street,
  Back of the Nuclear Mission,
Son of the town whore,
  Blamed television.

Justice, as usual, triumphed.
  Everyone felt fine.
Things went deader.
  Maloney went up the line.

Maloney learned one lesson:
  Never play the fool
With the products of especially a minor
  Public school.

Maloney lost a thing or two
  At that institution.
First shirt, second innocence,
  The old irresolution.

Found himself a girlfriend,
  Sharp suit, sharp collars.
Maloney on a moped,
  Pants full of dollars.

College boys on the corner
  In striped, strait blazers
Look at old Maloney,
  Eyes like razors.

'You don't need talent,' says Maloney.
  'You don't need looks.
All I got you got, fellers.
  You can keep your thick books.'

Parson got religion,
  Squire, in the end, the same.
The magistrate went over the wall.
  'Life,' said Maloney, ''s a game.'

Consider then the case of Maloney,
  College boys, parson, squire, beak.
Who was the victor and who was the victim?
  Speak.

over the wall: to gaol; sentenced to detention barracks

THE BALLAD OF BILLY OF NOSEY BENT
or HOW TO MAKE A POET

WHEN I was born at Nosey Bent
They watched the windows and raised the rent
They hung out my parents' wedding line
To see if I'd paid my nine-month fine
And when they found I'd overspent
They said my father was impotent.

When I went out on the patch to play
The village children ran away
Salt was my hair as the sea-bay sand
And I'd seven fingers on each hand
My face was white as the workhouse wall
And I wore my head like a cannon-ball.

While the children danced all over the hill
I cut the corn with Looney Lil
She didn't know what was three times seven
But she unscrewed her eyes and showed me heaven
I pillowed my head on her wounded breast
And the sun baled out in the bleeding west.

When the leaf lay light on the sycamore stem
They tried to send me to Bethlehem
The King of Passion, the Queen of Pain
Danced in their tower and lanced my brain
Trapped my tongue in a silver bit
That I might neither speak nor spit.

They said I would neither sing nor say
But young Prince Hamlet came my way
And took me to his house to dine
On salads of lilies and ballads of wine
Till I cast my cloak on the curling snow
Where the naked neighbours of Nosey go.

The Count of Nosey has a coat of mail
  But I fly feathered like the nightingale
Cold is my cage as death's bright dart
  But my walls stand soft as a poor man's heart
Three Wise Men wait at my garden gate
  My crown is crooked, but my jacket is strait.

THREE GIPSIES

THREE gipsies stood at my drifted door,
One was rich and one was poor
And one had the face of a blackamoor.

Out of the dark and the moor they came,
One was leaping, two were lame,
And each called out to me my name.

'Is there a baby that wants within
A penny of brass and a crown of tin
And a fire of spice for original sin?

'Hold him high at the window wide
That we may beg for him a Bride
From the circling star that swings outside.'

'Rise up, rise up, you gipsies three
Your baskets of willow and rush I see
And the third that is made of the Judas tree.

'No boy is born in my bed this day
Where the icicle fires her freezing ray,
For my love has risen and run away.

'So fare you well, Egyptians three,
Who bow and bring to me the key
From the cells of sin to set us free.'

Out of the million-angeled sky
As gold as the hairs of my head and thigh
I heard a new-born baby cry.

'Come back, come back, you gipsies three
And put your packs by my Christmas tree
For it is my son's nativity!'

Over the marble meadow and plain
The gipsies rode by the river's skein
And never more did they come again.

I set a star in the window tall,
The bread and wine in my waiting hall
And a heap of hay in the mangers all,

But the gipsies three with their gifts were gone,
And where the host of heaven had shone
The lunatic moon burned on, burned on.

BIBLE STORY

IN AUGUST, when the air of love was peeled,
I saw a burning boy upon the bed,
Shut a green shade against the harvest field
And held one shaking hand behind his head.

Stripped of his skin of breath, his heart untied,
I searched his threaded throat of serpentine,
And lying on the pallet at his side
I drew his beaten breast of milk to mine.

In this stone shell I poured such seas of prayer
His sailing soul was driven down from heaven,
His prodigal parents on the ringing stair
Heard, as the sun struck six, the boy sneeze seven,

And as he wandered, innocent, from my prison
Cried, *Hail, Elisha, for our son is risen!*

THE BALLAD OF CHARLOTTE DYMOND

Charlotte Dymond, a domestic servant aged eighteen, was murdered near Rowtor Ford on Bodmin Moor on Sunday 14 April 1844 by her young man: a crippled farm-hand, Matthew Weeks, aged twenty-two. A stone marks the spot.

IT WAS a Sunday evening
And in the April rain
That Charlotte went from our house
And never came home again.

Her shawl of diamond redcloth,
She wore a yellow gown,
She carried the green gauze handkerchief
She bought in Bodmin town.

About her throat her necklace
And in her purse her pay:
The four silver shillings
She had at Lady Day.

In her purse four shillings
And in her purse her pride
As she walked out one evening
Her lover at her side.

Out beyond the marshes
Where the cattle stand,
With her crippled lover
Limping at her hand.

Charlotte walked with Matthew
Through the Sunday mist,
Never saw the razor
Waiting at his wrist.

Charlotte she was gentle
But they found her in the flood
Her Sunday beads among the reeds
Beaming with her blood.

Matthew, where is Charlotte,
And wherefore has she flown?
For you walked out together
And now are come alone.

Why do you not answer,
Stand silent as a tree,
Your Sunday worsted stockings
All muddied to the knee?

Why do you mend your breast-pleat
With a rusty needle's thread
And fall with fears and silent tears
Upon your single bed?

Why do you sit so sadly
Your face the colour of clay
And with a green gauze handkerchief
Wipe the sour sweat away?

Has she gone to Blisland
To seek an easier place,
And is that why your eye won't dry
And blinds your bleaching face?

'Take me home!' cried Charlotte,
'I lie here in the pit!
A red rock rests upon my breasts
And my naked neck is split!'

Her skin was soft as sable,
Her eyes were wide as day,
Her hair was blacker than the bog
That licked her life away.

Her cheeks were made of honey,
  Her throat was made of flame
Where all around the razor
  Had written its red name.

As Matthew turned at Plymouth
  About the tilting Hoe,
The cold and cunning constable
  Up to him did go:

'I've come to take you, Matthew,
  Unto the magistrate's door.
Come quiet now, you pretty poor boy,
  And you must know what for.'

'She is as pure,' cried Matthew,
  'As is the early dew,
Her only stain it is the pain
  That round her neck I drew!

'She is as guiltless as the day
  She sprang forth from her mother.
The only sin upon her skin
  Is that she loved another.'

They took him off to Bodmin,
  They pulled the prison bell,
They sent him smartly up to heaven
  And dropped him down to hell.

All through the granite kingdom
  And on its travelling airs
Ask which of these two lovers
  The most deserves your prayers.

And your steel heart search, Stranger,
  That you may pause and pray
For lovers who come not to bed
  Upon their wedding day,

But lie upon the moorland
  Where stands the sacred snow
Above the breathing river,
  And the salt sea-winds go.

CHRIST AT THE CHEESEWRING

As I walked on the wicked moor
Where seven smashed stones lie
I met a man with a skin of tan
And an emerald in his eye.

All naked was his burning back
And naked was his thigh,
His only cloak it was the smoke
Out of the failing sky.

O loudly did he nail my name
Upon the mine-stacks three
And louder rose the ragged crows
That sail above the sea.

O will you drink my body deep
And wash my five wounds dry
That shot with snow now gravely grow
As scarlet as the sky?

All down, he said, *the drowning day*
And down the damaged sky
God's naked son his fingers won
About my thieving eye,

And like a bough about my brow
Planted a hand of horn
That men may see mirrored in me
The image of the thorn.

'I see no badge upon your brow
I drink no five wounds dry
I see no thief wrecked on the reef
Where seven smashed stones lie.'

Cheesewring: a granite cairn, thirty feet high, at the south-east corner of Bodmin Moor in Cornwall

Above the stone, above the sun,
Above the swinging sky
The King of Heaven the days seven
Is hanging out to die!

Softly he touched my turning head
And softly touched my side
And blessed with bread the waters red
That on the sea-bay slide.

I saw him climb the canvas sun
The strapped world to untie,
On its sharp strand with splintered hand
The flags of heaven fly.

I scattered in a sand of stars
His hand, his lip, his thigh,
I plucked the thorn that he had worn
Above his beating eye.

And on the land where seven stones stand
He stretched his hand to me
And on my brow of staring snow
Printed a gallows-tree.

CHILD'S SONG

Christopher Beer
  Used to live here,
Where the white water
  Winds over the weir,
Close to the claw
  Of the pawing sea,
Under the spear
  Of a cypress tree.

Never a nightingale
  Rings on the bough,
Burned is the orchard
  And broken the plough.
Out of the orient
  Light like a lash
Severed the sky
  And the river ran ash.

Over the valley
  Dawdled the fire
Swallowing city
  Steeple and spire,
All the proud people
  Nowhere to hide
Kindling flowers
  Of flame as they died.

Nobody passes
  Nor sheds a salt tear,
No one wears mourning
  For Christopher Beer:
Free as the fountain,
  Green as a gun,
Rich as the rainbow
  And blind as the sun.

THREE MASTS

THREE masts has the thrusting ship,
  Three masts will she wear
When she like Christ our Saviour
  Walks on the watery stair.

One stands at the fore
  To meet the weather wild
As He who once in winter
  Was a little child.

One grows after
  From step to the sky
For Him who once was keel-hauled
  And hung up to die.

One stands amidships
  Between fore and mizzen
Pointing to Paradise
  For Him who is risen.

Three masts will grow on the green ship
  Before she quits the quay,
For Father, Son, and Holy Ghost:
  Blessed Trinity.

DEATH OF A PUPIL

Now that you leave me for that other friend,
Rich as the rubbed sun, elegant of eye,
Who watched, in lost light, your five fortunes end
And wears the weapons of the wasted sky,

Often, I say, I saw him at your gate,
Noted well how he passed the time of day,
Gazed, with bright greed, at your young man's estate
And how, in fear, I looked the other way.

For we had met, this thief and I, before
On terrible seas, at the spoiled city's heart,
And when I saw him standing at your door
Nothing, I knew, could put you now apart.

O with sly promises he stroked the air,
Struck, on the coin of day, his gospel face.
I saw you turn, touch his hand, unaware
Of his thorned kiss or of his grave embrace.

GUY FAWKES' DAY

I AM the caught, the cooked, the candled man
With flames for fingers and whose thin eyes fountain,
I send on the stiff air my shooting stare
And at my shoulder bear the burning mountain.

I open on the dark my wound of speeches,
With stabs, with stars its seven last words wear,
My tongue of torches with the salamander
Breeds conversaziones of despair.

Milled in the minted light my skin of silver
Now curls, now kindles on the thicket's bone,
And fired with flesh in sepulchres of slumber
Walks the white night with sparks and showers sown.

At my fixed feet soldiers my coat of carbon
Slit with the speared sky. Their sacked eyes scan
My mask of medals. In bright mirrors of breath
Our faces fuse in death. My name is man.

SAILORS ASLEEP IN A CINEMA

ON SHORES of celluloid the sailors lie,
Caps piled in slices as life's bread and clay,
Dreaming of shirts and steaks, the polished thigh,
And sleep the giant actor's wars away.

One with pale throat thrown back and drifting limb
As for the naked dagger bares his breath;
Head on wrung hands or at an oppo's arm, they swim
In attitudes of innocence or death.

Or on a primitive Italian sea
They glide within the grove of spinning smoke,
Stunned, as Christ's seamen in Gethsemane,
The darkness dragged about them like a cloak.

O in such easy postures of defeat
My comrades keep their violent vigils still,
Wear in salt air the water's weather-sheet
And stir beneath the ocean's heavy hill.

Ice tries the trim, the tropic air for size.
The burst sun, scarred with burning birds, is gone.
Before our driven and disregarding eyes
Images sweat. The winding world roars on.

JOHNNY ALLELUIA

JOHNNY ALLELUIA
  In a seven-year cell
Watched the walking morning
  Didn't feel well,
Stretched for a string
  Of the leaping light,
Nailed it to his neck-bone
  Tacked it tight.

Up went Johnny
  In the blue, bold air,
You should have seen
  The screws all stare.
'Johnny?' they said,
  'More lives than a cat.
Never should have thought he'd done
  A thing like that.'

Johnny was a tinker
  Tramped to thc fair,
His kettles as bright
  As his tinplate hair.
With his tongue of chicken
  And his breast of ham
Johnny didn't give
  A tinker's damn.

It was 'Good old Johnny,'
  And 'Johnny here's the key,'
And 'Johnny put your hand
  Where it shouldn't be.'
O the girls all laughed
  And the boys didn't care
When Johnny came up
  Their kitchen stair.

But what is this blade
And what is this stone,
And why don't you take
A wife of your own?
Why do you wear
Your breeches so tight,
And what is this drum
Of dynamite?

'I sharpen my knife
On the winding stone
To cut me an apple
From the branch of bone.
My pants so tight
Keep my legs apart,
And I blast with powder
The human heart.'

Is this a bunch
Of skeleton keys,
And what is this wax
Under your chemise?
Why are your eyes
So clear, my son,
And you still under
Twenty-one?

'Under my shirt
My keys and my wax
Unlock the body
And silence the cracks.
I hear in my heart
The gold blood gad
As it did in the days
When Adam was a lad.'

It was 'Now then, Johnny,'
  And 'Johnny take care,
For boys like you
  There's nothing to spare.
In the lake of love
  You're sure to drown,
You can't walk on water
  In this town.

'You must keep your fingers
  To yourself
And your lollipop eye
  From another man's shelf.
And Johnny don't take
  Too long a pull
At all things bright
  And beautiful.'

They shanghai'd Johnny
  In a squinting cell
With modern plumbing
  And a view of hell.
They disinfected
  His public parts
And sketched his soul
  On little charts.

So he cast off shore
  And swung to sea.
The Governor wept,
  He said, said he,
'It was ever thus!'
  And shook his head.

'I'm damned if it was,'
  Young Johnny said.

GRAVE BY THE SEA

BY THE crunching, Cornish sea
Walk the man and walk the lover,
Innocent as fish that fare
In the high and hooking air,
And their deaths discover.

Beneath, you said, this turning tree,
With granite eye and stare of sand,
His heart as candid as the clay,
A seaman from the stropping bay
Took to the land.

Once this calmed, crystal hand was free
And rang the changes of the heart:
Love, like his life, a world wherein
The white-worm sin wandered not in.
Death played no part.

Wreathed, and with ringing fingers he
Passed like a prince upon the day
And from its four and twenty towers
Shot with his shaft the haggard hours,
Hauled them away.

So he set from the shaken quay
His foot upon the ocean floor
And from the wanting water's teeth
The ice-faced gods above, beneath,
Spat him ashore.

Now in the speaking of the sea
He waits under this written stone,
And kneeling at his freezing frame
I scrub my eye to see his name.

And read my own.

BY ST THOMAS WATER

BY St Thomas Water
Where the river is thin
We looked for a jam-jar
To catch the quick fish in.
Through St Thomas Churchyard
Jessie and I ran
The day we took the jam-pot
Off the dead man.

On the scuffed tombstone
The grey flowers fell,
Cracked was the water,
Silent the shell.
The snake for an emblem
Swirled on the slab,
Across the beach of sky the sun
Crawled like a crab.

'If we walk,' said Jessie,
'Seven times round,
We shall hear a dead man
Speaking underground.'
Round the stone we danced, we sang,
Watched the sun drop,
Laid our heads and listened
At the tomb-top.

Soft as the thunder
At the storm's start
I heard a voice as clear as blood,
Strong as the heart.
But what words were spoken
I can never say,
I shut my fingers round my head,
Drove them away.

'What are those letters, Jessie,
Cut so sharp and trim
All round this holy stone
With earth up to the brim?'
Jessie traced the letters
Black as coffin-lead.
'*He is not dead but sleeping*,'
Slowly she said.

I looked at Jessie,
Jessie looked at me,
And our eyes in wonder
Grew wide as the sea.
Past the green and bending stones
We fled hand in hand,
Silent through the tongues of grass
To the river strand.

By the creaking cypress
We moved as soft as smoke
For fear all the people
Underneath awoke.
Over all the sleepers
We darted light as snow
In case they opened up their eyes,
Called us from below.

Many a day has faltered
Into many a year
Since the dead awoke and spoke
And we would not hear.
Waiting in the cold grass
Under a crinkled bough,
Quiet stone, cautious stone,
What do you tell me now?

THE VISIT

THE poet at my door, Athenian-eyed,
Examined me, cautiously gave his hat,
Accepted a large whisky, failed to hide
His well-bred pain at my un-Celtic chat.

Combers of boiling hair crashed on his brow.
The voice was cool and, like the verse, unsweet,
Yet on the reasonable air, somehow,
Unorthodox Greek bells rang and drums beat.

What should have been my part remained unclear:
My thoughts, perhaps, too reverent, legs too weak.
Your smile was snow, yet all you seemed to hear
Was the one word I knew I must not speak.

You watched us, through the clear glass of your sun,
Exclaim upon your elegance, wit, skill,
And (opening up a naked heart) each one
Advancing into close range for the kill.

The only one who on this holy day
Dishonoured us was my old warrior cat,
Who, while the rest kissed heart and hand away,
Backed, metal-whiskered, to the wall and spat.

Its tail a flower of wires, its mask a blur,
It bared a thousand teeth, switched off its breath,
And with erect and all-electric fur
Ran sweating off as if your name was death.

Sex and the heat are equally to blame,
We said, and shut the spectre from the feast,
And when you went as silent as you came,
Noted how gently you forgave the beast.

We talked all night; long hoped you'd reappear
On serious, winged feet, vaulting from space,
Spoke of the charms with which you turned our fear,
And how old Tom the cat was our disgrace.

Yet, trudging later through your arctic prose
So widely praised for accuracy, grace,
Apparently our blood had failed, hearts froze,
And each of us had worn another face.

'What happened to the Greek?' my brothers said.
'At such unstinting love how could we fight?'
The things you wrote, of course, they never read:
Only I know the gospel cat was right.

RESERVOIR STREET

In 1926, the year
Of the Strike, on a day of bubbling heat
I went to stay with my sun-faced cousins
Who lived in a house on Reservoir Street.

Auntie stood strong as the Eddystone Lighthouse.
A terrible light shone out of her head.
Her children scuttled like ships for harbour.
'You must let them know what's what,' she said.

Her five prime-beef boys circled round me.
They didn't enjoy what they saw at all.
We couldn't make any more of each other
Than the map of stains on the bedroom wall.

All night long on the road to the city
The motor-car tyres rubbed out the dark.
Early in the morning I watched from the window
The sun like a killer come out of the park.

Down in the reservoir I saw a man drowning.
His flooding head came over the side.
They poked him out of a parcel of water.
'He's poisoned the drink!' my cousins cried.

I packed my bag and I said to Auntie,
'I think I'll go home on the one o'clock train.'
'My,' they all said, 'he wants his mammy.'
They never let me forget it again.

Through the Cornish jungle-country
Like a parrot the train screamed home.
I thought of my brother who slept beside me,
Four walls round us pure as cloam.

cloam: the clay used for making an earthenware oven (for baking bread etc.) built into the side of an old-fashioned open hearth

When I got to the house my head was thunder.
The bed lay open as a shell.
Sweet was my brother's kiss, and sweeter
The innocent water from the well.

SCHOOL AT FOUR O'CLOCK

AT FOUR o'clock the building enters harbour.
All day it seems that we have been at sea.
Now, having lurched through the last of the water,
We lie, stone-safe, beside the jumping quay.
The stiff waves propped against the classroom window,
The razor-back of cliffs we never pass,
The question-mark of green coiling behind us,
Have all turned into cabbages, slates, grass.

Up the slow hill a squabble of children wanders
As silence dries the valley like a drought,
When suddenly that speechless cry is raging
Once more round these four walls to be let out.
Like playing cards the Delabole slates flutter,
The founding stone is shaken in its mine,
The faultless evening light begins to stutter
As the cry hurtles down the chimney-spine.

Packing my bag with useless bits of paper
I wonder, when the last word has been said,
If I'd prefer to find each sound was thudding
Not round the school, but just inside my head.
I watch where the street lamp with sodium finger
Touches the darkening voices as they fall.
Outside? Inside? Perhaps either condition's
Better than his who hears nothing at all.

And I recall another voice. A teacher
Long years ago, saying, *I think I know*
Where all the children come from, but the puzzle
To me is, as they grow up, where they go?
Love, wonder, marvellous hope. All these can wither
With crawling years like flowers on a stalk;
Or, to some Piper's tune, vanish for ever
As creatures murdered on a morning walk.

Though men may blow this building up with powder,
Drag its stone guts to knacker's yard, or tip,
Smash its huge heart to dust, and spread the shingle
By the strong sea, or sink it like a ship—
Listen. Through the clear shell of air the voices
Still strike like water from the mountain bed;
The cry of those who to a certain valley
Hungry and innocent came. And were not fed.

CONDUCTING A CHILDREN'S CHOIR

THEY HOLD before their faces masks of flowers.
Their summer eyes anticipate the snow.
In skin as yet untouched by ticking showers
There lies the simple statement of the crow.

Meanwhile an audience, quite unaware
Of certain cunning, ancient as the Cave,
Observes the seraphim on sands of prayer,
Oblivious of each black, unbalanced wave.

The voices scale the trim, Italian airs,
Assail the senses with a brilliant pain.
Under my palm a calm corruption wears
An innocence articulate as rain.

I bait the snapping breath, curled claw, the deep
And delicate tongue that lends no man its aid.
The children their unsmiling kingdoms keep,
And I walk with them, and I am afraid.

WALKING

WALKING the lane's long-grave, the day
Fresh-dug with flowers and grasses thick
I felt the air with may turn sick,
And at the scent, and at the sound
Of water fighting from the ground,
Time and the hour thinned away.

You stood there: the same crackling dress
And that antique, huge-buttoned coat,
Brooch clear as coal pinned at your throat,
The lively hair caught in a bun,
Your face pecked by the clucking sun,
The voice as cool as watercress.

Straw hat, umbrella sleek and spread;
But neither one of these could hold
The storm that broke inside your head
Or keep you from the final cold.
And now the earth is on your face
And I am in another place.

Here, children by an altered moor
Stamp suds of may on a green floor
As under waving skies a trawl
Of hawthorn drags the orchard wall.
Slowly the sun winks a gilt eye.
Birds, dark as history, lumber by.

A SHORT LIFE OF NEVIL NORTHEY BURNARD

Cornish sculptor, 1818–1878

HERE lived Burnard who with his finger's bone
Broke syllables of light from the moorstone,
Spat on the genesis of dust and clay,
Rubbed with sure hands the blinded eyes of day,
And through the seasons of the talking sun
Walked, calm as God, the fields of Altarnun.

Here, where St Nonna with a holy reed
Hit the bare granite, made the waters bleed,
Madmen swam to their wits in her clear well,
Young Burnard fasted, watched, learned how to tell
Stone beads under the stream, and at its knock
Quietly lifted out his prize of rock.

As Michelangelo by stone possessed
Sucked the green marble from his mother's breast
So Burnard, at his shoulder the earth's weight,
Received on his child's tongue wafers of slate
And when he heard his granite hour strike
Murdered Christ's hangman with a mason's spike.

The village sprawled white as a marriage bed,
Gulls from the north coast stumbled overhead
As Burnard, standing in the churchyard hay,
Leaned on the stiff light, hacked childhood away,
On the tomb slabs watched bugler, saint, dove,
Under his beating fists grow big with love.

The boy with the Laocoön's snake crown
Caught with a six-inch nail the stinking town.
He turned, as Midas, men to stone, then gold.
Forgot, he said, what it was to be cold.
Birds rang like coins. He spread his fingers wide.
Wider the gulfs of love as his child died.

Packing only his heart, a half-hewn stone,
He left house, clothes, goods, blundered off alone:
London to Cornwall and the spinning moor,
Slept in stacks, hedges, barns, retraced the spoor
Of innocence; through the lost shallows walked,
Of his dead child, they say, for ever talked.

At last, the dragged November sun on high,
Burnard lay in a mumpers' inn to die.
At Redruth Workhouse, with the stripped, insane,
Banged on death's door and did not bang in vain;
Rocked in a gig to sleep in paupers' clay
Where three more warmed his side till judgement day.

No mourner stood to tuck him in God's bed,
Only the coffin-pusher. Overhead,
The fishing rooks unravelling the hour,
Two men, a boy, restored Camborne Church tower.
'This box,' the clerk said, 'holds your man in place.'
'We come,' they said, 'to smooth dirt from his face.'

No cross marks the spot where he first saw day.
Time with a knife wears the dull flesh away,
Peels the soft skin of blocks cut on the green
Signed by a boy, *Burnard. Sculptor. Thirteen.*
Slowly the land shakes as the ocean's gun
Sounds over Cornwall. He stares from the sun.

The torn tramp, rough with talents, walks the park.
Children have swift stones ready. Men, dogs, bark.
The light falls on the bay, the cold sea leaks,
The slate face flushes, opens its lips, speaks.
In from the moor the pointing shadows flock,
Finger, beneath the river, the pure rock.

TRUSHAM

IN THIS blown house my grandfather was born,
And here his father first unshook his bones.
Walking the churchyard as a child, I saw
My slate name on their double page of stones.

The War Memorial—a lump of rock,
Upended rollers, length of iron twine—
Crests like a coaster the hill's wave. I read
The bullet-coloured names. My father's. Mine.

In Rattle Street the mud is Flanders-thick.
An old man, shoulder-sacked against the rain
Under the dropping fingers of a rick
Asks, 'What is it that brings you here again?

'You never married, and you've got no child
(I don't know what your dad would say to that)
And you the only one. It seems to me
That when you've gone, the name will just go scat.'

How can I tell him that the sounding heart—
Oiled with the same old blood—can't be reset?
Useless to say that this particular flesh
Won't scrape off, dry off, like the mud, the wet.

Beyond those pale disturbances of sky
Another year assembles its vast floe.
Ice lines the turning air. It softens. Soon
Advances from the west the carrion snow.

HOSPITAL

HOSPITAL is the war again.
I left my clothes somewhere in town.
Here I am innocent and good.
I watch the doctor. A slight frown.
I watch myself in his white gaze
Anxiously doing all he says.
'Breathe in. Drink this. Say Ah. Lie down.'

The ward is like a warship's mess:
Washed, painted, laid out like a bride.
Against the bulkhead, monsters press.
Fears through the drifting garden glide.
Elsewhere, through blinding deserts, snow,
The vulnerable peoples go,
But we're as safe as hell inside.

Close by, two old companions stand,
Affectionate, attentive still.
They grasp my hand with self-same joy—
One dressed to cure, one dressed to kill,
Though which is which I cannot say
Until the light drags in the day
Over the burden of the hill.

DEMOLITION ORDER

WHAT do I remember of my home town?
  I remember Ma Treloar
Hanging blankets, sheets, for banners
  Over a measled kitchen door
That no matter how early I went by,
  The dawn's uproar not begun,
Always gaped expectantly
  As if waiting to admit the sun.

Fate in its unlusting time
  Hadn't responded to Ma Treloar with roses,
Preferring instead to dispense
  Several doses.
Still, she looked well on it:
  Better, it seemed to me,
Than the respectable dead who paraded the town,
  Already of, though not yet in, the cemetery.

Behind Ma Treloar, a rubble of children:
  Loins like catapults,
(True love, it was whispered in my home town,
  Always produced the same enviable results);
Voices like fire engines, manners like goats,
  They drank each other's tears, careless as showers,
Fought and danced like fleas,
  Wore insults for flowers.

They lay in the swarming air
  In attitudes of terrible relaxation,
Enjoying with dogs, trees, birds, beds, fire,
  Some secret and indefinable relation,
Rubbed casually each other's thighs, lay in one
    another's crutches
  With an apparent lack of emotion,
Swam tenderly in their mother's love like sprats
  In an enveloping ocean.

In all joys and calamities Ma Treloar would be there
  Handing out wine and bread,
Beating beaks, archbishops, the Welfare, to it.
  Now that the old girl's dead,
Her stinking house bashed down and eaten by
    bulldozers
  Outside the town wall,
I feel something else has been quietly brained,
    dragged out
  Of the universe; an atmosphere of the Fall.

Now that I'm old enough (foolish enough?) to know
    better
  I dare say if she returned, she'd merely
Set the same disaster-markers at the street corner
  Nodding and sounding just as clearly,
And continue to frighten the guts out of solitaries
  Like most of us, as so often before.
But was it, I can't help wondering, a pity
  That she was a whore?

It was strictly Ma Treloar's function,
  Inevitably that of the tart,
To provide the homeless with home, the nameless
    with name,
  The heartless with heart;
To open her house like a warm stone fan
  Under the castle's torn crag,
To stand in the doorway, to show neither hope nor
    despair
  As the yellow day spread its flag.

'Lord, man,' she'd say, 'but you've certainly
  Grown thinner,'
As the prophet of the desert, having eaten nothing
    but sand and prayers for a week
  Arrived for Sunday dinner,
Leaving his taut, ex-ravening lion with its umbrella
    of bones and skin
  At the foot of the stair,
Doves descending on its pecked head as it lay
  With the gentle vulture, the lynx, the once
    wild-eyed hare.

DOCKACRE

TWO doors away, at Dockacre, a ghost
In an isosceles cap assembles just before dawn,
Jerks round the ripped garden, through the dog-gates
And up the buckled stairs, quietly playing a flute.

Often, sleepless in a bland electric glare
(Since I slept on the mess-deck, to wake up
Without a pilot-light gives me the feeling
I'm going to be drowned) I've tried to hear it

Rounding the hollyhocks for the front door, but so far
It's always been the paper-train. The ghost's name
Is Nicholas Herle, once High Sheriff of Cornwall.
On the wall at Dockacre there's a creamy portrait of the wife

Who was shot by accident, stabbed, or driven mad,
No one seems quite certain which, though probably
It was the last. In a curled account
He shut the girl in a dark room, trying

To starve her to sanity. She died of the cure
On Christmas Day 1714, and Nicholas left for Hampstead,
But we've never forgotten her, or him.
My neighbour still has the bald flute. It's part

Of a cane walking-stick. He kindly offered
To play it to me once, but I declined,
Fearing that I might hear it again in the chopped hours:
Nicholas playing his inaccurate, sad tunes

As I whistled mine; both of us suffering from the same
Malaise that evidently even death won't cure.
I feared that as I looked towards my bedroom door
I should see the handle break slowly into flames, then
turn.

A LOCAL HAUNTING

Botathen, near Launceston, Cornwall

ONLY one person knew her well:
The farmer's youngest, innocent son
Who, schoolwards, homewards, white as hail,
Would see her, break into a run,
To deaf ears tell his sweating tale.
There seems no doubt she gave him hell.

With the calm light her hands she'd lave,
Walking the clean, unprinted sand,
As from her shoulders fell a shawl
And the gaunt ring fell from her hand,
So the boy's tears each day would fall,
For he had seen her in her grave.

She crossed his vision like a snow
That he, and only he, could spy,
At noonday's heat, at morning's chill,
Wherever he might stand or lie
She kept her silent watch until
Light from the day began to flow.

Why she should choose him none could tell,
Or if she lay within his head.
At all events, he lost his grin,
Woke naked, screaming, in his bed,
Refused to speak, to eat, grew thin
While the frail shade grew strong and well.

Family, neighbours, turned aside.
Trembling, he thumbed his bible page,
Hearing men speak of Bedlam, where
—Twice-locked within the human cage—
He knew he'd find her, waiting there
To lie beside him like a bride.

At last, the rook-tailed priest, his wits
Propped with a rowan stick, a brass
Ring on his finger, creaking mouth
Of prayers, cut a raw star of grass,
Stood, as the custom, to the south,
Piously blew the ghost to bits.

What were the words she tried in vain
To speak to a child's unbruised heart?
The priest in his confessor's head
Kept her slow stain of speech apart,
And the boy's father, it was said,
Looked, somehow, more himself again.

And the sun rose, dispelled the vague
Irrelevant mist above the stream.
Softly the boy unclenched his fear.
His mother smiled, placid as cream:
In 1665, the year
Of the spruce, dog-eyed king, the Plague.

Yet all his life, with stiffening brow,
He waited for the ghost's return,
Paced the untenanted field. Afraid,
Alone, abstracted, he would burn
With love for the bitch of a shade,
Attend her voice, as I do now.

DEATH OF A POET

SUDDENLY his mouth filled with sand.
His tractor of blood stopped thumping.
He held five icicles in each hand.
His heart packed up jumping.

His face turned the colour of something forgotten in the larder.
His thirty-two teeth were expelled on the kitchen floor.
His muscles, at long last, got considerably harder.
He felt younger than he had for some time before.

Four heroes, steady as wrestlers, each carried him on a shoulder
Into a great grey church laid out like a brain.
An iron bowl sent out stiff rays of chrysanthemums. It grew colder.
The sun, as expected, failed to break through the pane.

The parson boomed like a dockyard gun at a christening.
Somebody read from the bible. It seemed hours.
I got the feeling you were curled up inside the box, listening.
There was the thud of hymn-books, the stench of flowers.

I remembered hearing your voice on a bloody foment
Of Atlantic waters. The words burned clear as a flare.
Life begins, you said, *as of this moment.*
A bird flew down out of the hurling air.

Over the church a bell broke like a wave upended.
The hearse left for winter with a lingering hiss.
I looked in the wet sky for a sign, but no bird descended.
I went across the road to the pub; wrote this.

THE QUESTION

IN THE locked sky beats a dove.
It speaks continually of love.

Deep in the river a talking stone
Says he lies easy who lies alone.

Under the stone there hides a knife:
The beginning and end of every life.

In the dark forest are flowers of light
That never fade by day or night.

Down in the valley stands a tree,
Its roots uneasy as the sea.

High on the tree there hangs a nest.
Here, says the wind, *you must take your rest*.

Through the spinney with eyes of wax
Runs the woodman with glaring axe.

Naked, my love and I arise
Bathed in his fearful prophecies.

Whose is the bird and whose the stone,
Whose is the light on the midnight sown?

Whose is the tree and whose the rest,
And whose is the knife upon my breast?

Who is the woodman and what does he cry?
Gaze in the mirror. Do not reply.

IN COVENTRY

In Coventry, that ruddled city,
Under a metal, shunting sky,
I sat in the cracked cathedral,
The holiday-makers limping by.

Christ hung down like a hawk-moth caterpillar,
Down his cheeks ran woollen tears.
On the chapel gate his crown of thorns
Was made by the Royal Engineers.

As I walked through the glittering Precinct
All the retables burned like gold.
I heard a gear-change of bones behind me.
I saw a man lying, flat out, cold.

He hit the slabs as though he'd been sandbagged.
A thicket of blood sprang on his face.
We looked for a seat to lay him out on,
But man must keep moving in that place.

The rain fell down the concrete mountain.
Four friends came back, breathing hard.
'Pull yourself together, Taff,' they chuntered.
But his legs were butter and his face was lard.

'Taff, don't let us down,' they were saying.
Taff looked dead and half-buried already,
As on a river of whisky he'd taken
The quickest way out of Coventry city.

Later, on a weir of steps, I saw him
Stumbling, alone; past hopes and fears.
The blood and hair on his jagged brow
Held in place by the engineers.

A VISIT TO STRATFORD

HIGH IN the Warwickshire sky the immaculate sun
Squeezed a thin heat as the weed and the water coiled
Round the arches of Clopton Bridge, the fed-up swans.
My mind was elsewhere, for love—like the spring—had
  cooled.

It wasn't the lack of love, but the reason why
That sucked at my thoughts as the river the turning stone.
Prince Hamlet, green as a penny, heaved a bronze sigh.
Branches flickered with coins. A lean wind sniffed for
  your bone.

Rows of coaches, in dangerous colours, lay round the
  park
Like out of date monsters anticipating the snow.
A tree someone said you were said to have planted
  burned dark,
Seemed to grope the strong earth for you, seventeen feet
  below.

I thought, at the Birthplace, I'd still find you resident
  there
Along with the cradle, the verse safe as germs under
  glass.
All I could see was a hole in a torrent of air,
Ringed by stiff, relevant flowers and too-tight grass.

I walked, when the Easter light had cautiously risen,
To touch the red hairs of your beard, your skin of pure
  stone,
But the church was locked, though Christ was out of his
  prison.
The thick river beat on the graveyard wall, lurched on.

In the orchard at Shottery, irreconcilable birds
Savaged, with innocent skill, the last of the day.
An army marched seven times round your city of words.
The cottage was silent; the sad, frantic ghosts were away.

Returning to Cornwall with nothing, as usual, to tell,
I slept and half-slept, and the trembling fire blazed clear.
The heart, in its zoo of ribs, healed; the soft night fell,
And a voice—it was your voice—spoke with the evening
  bell,

Why do you travel so far for what is most near?
The smallest coin in your purse buys what is most dear.

PORTRAIT

HE NEVER wrote a bad line in his life,
And never wrote a good one, come to that.
He started out stripped to the buff for strife,
But all that naked muscle turned to fat.

He never ventured on a cracking limb.
He caught, in crises, the last train but one,
And when the moon, the stars, appeared to dim,
Made no attempt to seize the whirling sun.

He blundered, roaring, through the silent wood.
He sprayed and pruned and cut it to the bone,
And when his children as the chopped saints stood,
Imagined all the blood to be his own.

He rode to battle on a clanking horse,
With similar rage fell on the weak, the strong,
Gazed on the bursting dead without remorse
And ate his supper up. Sang a loud song.

In letters eight feet high I watched him tell
The secret history of his bleeding heart.
Ice moved beneath his feet, and when snow fell
He slowly tore its mysteries apart.

Wearing a prize of scalps about his belt
He knelt at last upon the woodland ride,
Stripping the animal poetry of its pelt,
Amazed to find that the poor bitch had died.

LORD SYCAMORE

I CLIMBED Lord Sycamore's castle,
  The wind was blowing red.
'Top of the morning, my lord,' I cried.
  'Top to you,' he said.

'Welcome to Sycamore Castle,'
  His smile as sharp as tin,
'Where many broken men come out
  That in one piece go in.'

With pusser's eggs and bacon
  My belly it was rare.
'Together,' said Lord Sycamore,
  'Let's take the dancing air.'

With a running finger
  He chucked me under the chin.
Felt with a lover's quiet hand
  Where he might best begin.

Suddenly he cooled me
  As we laughed and joked.
Although the month was May, my breath
  On the morning smoked.

On the sum of my body
  Lord Sycamore got to work,
Pulled the answer like a rose
  Out of my mouth with a jerk.

On Lord Sycamore's castle
  I heard the morning stop;
Over my head, the springing birds,
  Under my feet, the drop.

A CERTAIN MAN

COMING down Ridgegrove Hill, the charging wind
Dislodging slate clouds from the cliff of sky,
I saw a stranger by disaster pinned
To blood and granite where the stream scuds by.

His palms of silver bled with burning light.
Roses of blood broke at his throat, his thighs.
The scarlet insect of his tongue blazed bright.
The tall fly trudged the forest of his eyes.

Out of the sour dust I plucked the knife,
Held up his head, scooped his rich coins of breath;
Watched at his curling loins the proper life—
Blood cover up his nakedness with death.

'Tell me your name that I may now provide
Your parable with oil and wine and bread.'
'I am the Good Samaritan,' he cried,
Seizing my sharpened hand, my fingers red.

AFTER THE ACCIDENT

COVERING up his wounds with careful snow
He rose and walked back to the world of men.
'We thought,' they said, 'the day we saw you go
That we should never see your face again.

'The accident destroyed both hands, you say?
Broke your two legs and smashed, was it, your side?
And then to think, on that same wedding day,
Worse than the worst, that you should lose your
  bride.'

The surgeon, he replied, *a famous knight,*
Hardly stopped short at raising up the dead.
I think that you'll agree in any light
You'd never spot the scars about my head.

Observe how steady is my arm, my eye,
How sure my step, and see how firm my fists.
'We all agree,' they said, 'you're looking spry,
But is that blood that's running down your wrists?'

I never felt, he said, *so fighting fit.*
Such joy, at last, to have regained my powers!
'Physically, yes,' they cried, 'we must admit,
But why the grave-clothes and the scent of flowers?'

He lost the old, the eloquent appeal.
Friends looked away and love finally died,
For who, touching the Bridegroom, cares to feel
Holes in the hands and feet, except the Bride?

THE SHEEP ON BLACKENING FIELDS

THE SHEEP on blackening fields
No weather-warning know
As the thin, sapping sun
Annihilates the snow.
Winter has eased its grip,
The struck fountain flows;
Burns in its lamp of leaves
The white flame of the rose.

In the sharp river's gut
Fish and blurred stars unfreeze;
Unclench at the moor's side
The fists of trees.
Unscientifically housed
And in his hand a stone,
Grizzles in dusty hay
A naked child, alone.

A star of bitter red
Above the mountain crest
Writes on the squalling dark,
Christus natus est.
Silently we renew
The ruined bread and wine;
Take the huge-bellied child
Whose flesh is yours, is mine.

BALLAD OF THE BREAD MAN

MARY STOOD in the kitchen
  Baking a loaf of bread.
An angel flew in through the window.
  'We've a job for you,' he said.

'God in his big gold heaven,
  Sitting in his big blue chair,
Wanted a mother for his little son.
  Suddenly saw you there.'

Mary shook and trembled,
  'It isn't true what you say.'
'Don't say that,' said the angel.
  'The baby's on its way.'

Joseph was in the workshop
  Planing a piece of wood.
'The old man's past it,' the neighbours said.
  'That girl's been up to no good.'

'And who was that elegant fellow,'
  They said, 'in the shiny gear?'
The things they said about Gabriel
  Were hardly fit to hear.

Mary never answered,
  Mary never replied.
She kept the information,
  Like the baby, safe inside.

It was election winter.
  They went to vote in town.
When Mary found her time had come
  The hotels let her down.

The baby was born in an annexe
  Next to the local pub.
At midnight, a delegation
  Turned up from the Farmers' Club.

They talked about an explosion
  That made a hole in the sky,
Said they'd been sent to the Lamb & Flag
  To see God come down from on high.

A few days later a bishop
  And a five-star general were seen
With the head of an African country
  In a bullet-proof limousine.

'We've come,' they said, 'with tokens
  For the little boy to choose.'
Told the tale about war and peace
  In the television news.

After them came the soldiers
  With rifle and bomb and gun,
Looking for enemies of the state.
  The family had packed and gone.

When they got back to the village
  The neighbours said, to a man,
'That boy will never be one of us,
  Though he does what he blessed well can.'

He went round to all the people
  A paper crown on his head.
Here is some bread from my father.
  Take, eat, he said.

Nobody seemed very hungry.
  Nobody seemed to care.
Nobody saw the god in himself
  Quietly standing there.

He finished up in the papers.
  He came to a very bad end.
He was charged with bringing the living to life.
  No man was that prisoner's friend.

There's only one kind of punishment
  To fit that kind of a crime.
They rigged a trial and shot him dead.
  They were only just in time.

They lifted the young man by the leg,
  They lifted him by the arm,
They locked him in a cathedral
  In case he came to harm.

They stored him safe as water
  Under seven rocks.
One Sunday morning he burst out
  Like a jack-in-the-box.

Through the town he went walking.
  He showed them the holes in his head.
Now do you want any loaves? he cried.
  'Not today,' they said.

BALLAD OF THE FROG PRINCESS

A YOUNG prince rode the partridge wood,
  One hand on his bright thigh,
The other reined his sprinting mare
  As he passed by.
'Why do you range the woods,' I cried,
  'Where sullen thickets claw?
For unprotected is your heart,
  And your wounds raw.'

'Here I shall find my love,' he said,
  'For love did not find me
Upon the poisoned field of war
  Or on the sea,
And she will hold me in her arms,
  Search with a tender eye,
That my cleft heart again be one
  And my wounds dry.'

Long, long he rode the snapping brake
  Under a roof of spray,
And long I heard his bugle-horn
  At close of day,
Until the trees with leopard leaves
  Sprang softly into flame,
Ice silenced the loud waterfall
  And the snows came.

But when the fingers of the spring
  Had felt the dark earth through,
I met him by the forest oak
  In garments new.
As white as Sunday was his hair,
  His skin a wand new-peeled,
He bore no sword at his right hand,
  His wounds were healed.

'As through the heart's weather you rode,
  Prince, did you find your bride?'
The young man raised a sultry eye
  As he replied,
'I met my love as I was told
  Beneath the elder-tree,
But hers was not the face or form
  Long promised me.

'She lay upon the bridle-path,
  She gleamed upon a log,
Her eyes were two bold diamonds
  In a green frog,
And green and wet and wet and green
  To my cold hand she clung,
And crawled upon my murdered breast
  And kissed my tongue.

'She whispered to me as the sea,
  Entreated me to stay.
All things will change, she said, upon
  Our wedding day.
And so within my golden hand
  I hold the wedding ring,
Sleep all night in a double bed,
  And love is king.'

'Prince, when the forward morning through
  Your marriage window shone,
The white stars melting in the sky,
  The guests long gone,
You found that from your side the frog
  Had vanished like spring snow?
And in its place a loving bride?'

  'I do not know.'

DEVONPORT

Tune: 'The Streets of Laredo'

I SAW two sailors in Devonport city,
Their bones were of shell and their eyes were marine.
'Never forget,' said the one to the other,
'The deeds we have done and the sights we have seen.'

As they came down Ker Street by Devonport Column,
By the Egyptian and Oddfellows' Hall,
No sound was heard from the Nile-voiced oracle,
Beak-faced, indifferent, marching the wall.

In the Old Chapel I sat with my doxy,
Down came the sun with its streamers of gin,
Down by the Forum a blind-fingered fiddler
Felt for a tune that was crazy as sin.

Empty the gallows-rope blew on the morning,
Empty your heart when you wake up in bed,
Stare in despair at the face there beside you,
Find that, like you, it is dead, it is dead.

I went down Fore Street, the summer descending,
Turning my voice on the rim of the tide,
'Do you recall how we three sailed together?'
'We never heard of you, mister,' they cried.

'Swore that whenever misfortune befell us
Nothing should sever the word I now speak?'
Only the wind shoving down from the Dockyard
Troubled the waters about Stonehouse Creek.

Old Chapel: pub in Devonport

Lightly they walked on the lap of the morning,
Their hair was of pitch and their tongues sweet as tar,
While high in the heaven a love-killed old kitehawk
Bawled on the blue like an opera star.

Blithely O blithely the casual morning
Burned life away as the leaf on a tree,
Rolling the sun like a mad hoop beside me,
And down at the end of the alley, the sea.

PELORUS JACK

AN ABRAHAM with a crystal jaw
Told me your story, and awoke
You in the streaming grave. I saw
You lift your wild head as he spoke.

You were the crewmen's dazzling boy
Who turned from life his wounded head;
Whom death with warm, uncasual eye
Nudged gently from his single bed.

I saw the eager, anxious crew,
The grumbling cliffs on either hand
Where the sea-channel slowly drew
Its snake of water through the sand.

Black flames of dark burned down the day,
The moon's gold pleasure-wheel was gone,
When from the hollows of the sea
A figure rose and led them on.

Through the trimmed waters of the strait
It swam, with fins of fire, ahead;
Brought the ship to the harbour-gate
And the young sea-boy from the dead.

An angel, so the sailors said,
With sacred smile and feathers bright,
Had through miraculous waters led
The boy into the healing light.

No angel led them through the dark
In answer to a crumbling prayer:
It was, my Abraham said, a shark
Bathing with phosphor the black air.

A shark that on its flaring back
Bore the young saint from night to day;
Seamen called it Pelorus Jack
And, hunting, looked the other way.

This I remember as the sun
Explodes; the cold sea fills the skies.
Into my mouth the waters run
And through the windows of my eyes.

And I am hauled from my soft blood.
I hear the vessel make for shore.
'Look!' all the seamen cry. 'The good
Fish rises on the sea once more!'

But I have seen that fish before.
Its teeth are sharp. Its throat is red.
It gives no light, and I can hear
The sea on the stabbed rocks ahead.

BALLAD OF JACK CORNWELL

John Travers Cornwell, 1st Class Boy, RN, sight-setter of the forecastle gun in HMS 'Chester', was mortally wounded at the Battle of Jutland, 31 May 1916. He was posthumously awarded the Victoria Cross. His age was under 16½ years.

I WOKE up one morning,
  Unwound my sheet of clay,
Lifted up my tombstone lid
  And asked the time of day.
I walked out one morning
  When the sun was dark
Left my messmates sleeping
  Deep in Manor Park.

In the Admiralty heaven
  Lurked the gods of war,
Waiting for young Jack Cornwell
  As they had once before.
High in the pusser's heaven
  The naked war gods hung,
With palpitating eye, stiff parts,
  And leaking tongue.

When I went down to Devonport
  My face was cold as slate,
They gave me a number for my name
  As I went through the barrack gate.
Round the banks of the dry dock
  Wandered the iron tree;
Close in its jacket of water
  Jerked the idiot sea.

When I came out of depot
  My heart was beating bright.
The lily bloomed in the valley,
  The holly flowers were white.
As we sailed to meet the enemy
  The history book looked raw,
John Jellicoe put on his golden arm,
  And Beatty his bulldog jaw.

Mother, don't watch for postie,
  I shan't have time to write,
I'm off to the Battle of Jutland,
  And there's no shore leave tonight.
Don't weep on the kitchen table
  If a letter I don't send.
Today is the Battle of Jutland
  And there won't be a make and mend.

Who are all those swimmers
  Knocking on our bulkhead,
Gazing face-down at their fortunes
  On the stone sea bed?
With the ramming waters
  They no longer toil.
Their breath is turned to quiet salt,
  And their lungs to oil.

Jellicoe: Admiral Sir John Jellicoe, C.-in-C., Grand Fleet, 1914–1916
Beatty: Vice-Admiral Sir David Beatty, Commander, 1st Battle Cruiser Squadron
postie: the postman
make and mend: a half-day's holiday

Suddenly around me
   The Gunnery Jacks all spoke
Their terrible words of gunpowder
   And sentences of smoke.
The deck blew up like a candle,
   I heard the Gunner's Mate say,
It looks more like November the fifth
   Than the thirty-first of May.

But the catherine wheels were made of iron,
   The stars were made of steel,
And downward came a scarring rain
   The sun will never heal.
Death came on like winter
   Through the water-gate.
All I could do by the forecastle gun
   Was stand alone, and wait.

Mother, all around me
   My freezing comrades lie,
And though to each I speak his name
   No one makes reply.
All around me, mother,
   Their coats of sleep they wear
As if for a long journey
   They must now prepare.

I put my hand in my flannel,
   The air was black, was red,
And when I pulled it out again
   I knew that I was dead.
They took me down to London,
   They launched me up the nave,
They sank me in a wooden boat
   Into a poor man's grave.

Gunnery Jacks: Gunnery Officers
flannel: seaman's shirt

They pinned a medal on my chest,
  And though my pillow was deep
They took the pennies off my eyes
  And lifted me from my sleep.
They gave me a second funeral,
  I heard the rifles plain
And up in the wild air went the birds
  As I went down again.

The great Sir Edward Carson,
  First Lord of the Admiralty,
Asked men and women who grumbled
  If ever they heard of me.
It was the second year of the war:
  Thiepval, the Somme, Verdun.
The people were encouraged,

  And the Great War went on.

THE SENTINEL'S STORY

1805

After the Battle of Trafalgar the body of Lord Nelson was placed in a cask of brandy as the 'Victory' made for Gibraltar. On the night of 24 October, owing to a displacement of air from the corpse, the lid of the cask burst open and the body reappeared. The rumour ran round the ship that the Admiral had risen from the dead.

THREE days below Trafalgar
  Walking the western swell,
Where in the Shoals of Peter
  Many deep-seamen dwell,
Our ship, wearing the weather,
  Taut as the travelling tree,
Now shook its hundred branches
  On forests of the sea.

The Captain in his cabin
  Slept in the walnut wood,
Jack Strop within his swinging bed,
  The nipper where he could.
Some slept above and some below
  The waving water-line,
But soundest slept the Admiral
  Buried in brandy-wine.

Jack Strop: truculent sailor
nipper: boy seaman (when weighing anchor, the cable was once secured to an endless rope by 'stoppers' or 'nippers', worked by ships' boys who became known by the latter name)

I saw the midnight turning
  That still, surrendered breath,
The good Lord Nelson burning
  Upon the reefs of death.
I saw him take the bullet
  Aboard his breast, his spine,
On his cocked coat of medals
  Spill the bright, bitter wine.

The marksman in his mizzen
  Fifteen salt yards away
Saw good Lord Nelson strolling
  About his bloody day.
The gunners they stood naked
  Upon their deadly drill,
But Nelson, cased in the gold-lace,
  Was dressed to kill, to kill.

Around his throat his ribbons,
  His high-hat on his head,
Mates, in that tiddley uniform
  He was already dead.
His five of decorations
  He ferried on the flood,
The four all made of silver
  And one all made of blood.

The water, wine and lemon
  They carried to his bed,
They rubbed his chest, they rubbed his breast,
  They shot his sniper dead.
Don't throw me overboard, he cried.
  How dear is life to men!
He opened up his pearly eyes
  And shut them down again.

They cropped for Lady Hamilton
  The harvest of his hair,
They put him in his pusser's shirt
  Within the leaguer there.
Around the ripened hour
  They cut for him a cape,
Stitched with the sacred spirit
  That's gathered from the grape.

On the October ocean
  Loud blew the bucking gale
As south towards Gibraltar
  Now swam the wooden whale,
And in her level belly
  No shake Lord Nelson feels,
The new wine pouring at his head,
  The old out at his heels.

But with the bell at midnight
  The good Lord Nelson stirred,
The breath within his body
  Burst in a long, last word.
The top jumped off the leaguer,
  He lifted up his head,
And pale as paint the seaman's saint
  Came driving from the dead.

leaguer: large barrel

O some were winding up their wounds,
  Some prayed, some played, some swore,
And some were saving up their strength
  For a dicky run ashore,
But when the Lord High Admiral
  Came dancing through the drum
Every man in *Victory*
  Thought his hour had come.

'We should have anchored,' Hardy said.
  'It was his last command!
I shouldn't be surprised, boys,
  If we don't get to land.'
But casting his caulked eye about
  His pale and chattering crew,
Lord Nelson sank within his tank.
  The sailing storm hove to.

Now wheeled about the changing moon,
  Now spun the little stars,
Soft as a wish flew the bright fish,
  Now slept the steady tars.
Now ran our ruined vessel
  Around the beating clock
And anchored with the weather
  Under the bully Rock.

So here's to good Lord Nelson
  Who from his spirit's den
Commanded wind and weather
  To save his fellow men.
And here's to the good brandy,
  Long may its blessings be
On us, and all who wander
  The grave and open sea.

IMMUNITY

LINING up with the naked sailors,
The smell of Africa blown offshore,
I watched the sweat run down to my ankles,
Borrowed a tickler from the man next door.

The sick-bay tiffy looked more like a doctor.
The quack was nervous, his face of bread;
He might have been last man in for England,
The sky gone dark and the pitch turned red.

'It's nothing,' he said as he dipped the needle,
Pumped it full of jungle juice.
'Don't look at the man in front, that's the secret.
It's not like putting your head through a noose.'

We stuck out our arms. He looked at his needle,
Showed the usual pusser's restraint,
Suddenly swallowed his oath to Hippocrates,
Fell on the deck in a number-one faint.

No one was issued with a jab at Freetown.
No one complained of feeling crook.
Malaria, yellow and blackwater fever
Lay down low till we pulled up the hook.

Rocked on the antiseptic ocean
Nobody noticed the turning screw.
'This could cost a fortune,' we said, 'in peace-time,
The sun so yellow and the sea so blue.'

quack: ship's medical officer
hook: anchor

And, for the record, off Kos a month later
Where Hippocrates lived out his term,
Most of them died of wounds or sea-water,
Including the doctor. None of a germ.

The physician Hippocrates once practised on the Greek island of Kos, which was also his birthplace.

LETTER TO POSEIDON

GREASING the gun or ditching the gash, I'd view
(A wrenching wind pulling my hand, my eye)
In your dissimilarities of blue
Sewage, scum, flowers slowly coiling by.

Although I knew you built the walls of Troy,
Could shrink five oceans to as many lakes,
I found your manner questionable, coy.
Frankly, your attitude gave me the shakes.

I wondered if, when gulped down by your sire,
You thought for one cracked moment you had died,
Only to find yourself face-down, entire,
Ejected on the stumbling mountainside.

And when the world burst like a rotten shoe
Your coat of clichés was the poets' hell,
With 'azure' as the only word for blue,
And spray, as usual, 'like diamonds' fell.

Often I used to watch you in your den
Humped like a sea-slug in your coral chair,
Your bloody trident stuck with ships and men,
The fish at anchor in your fattened hair.

You see, I never went for all that stuff
About your chariot, and the puffing stud
That runs in weather rare, in weather rough,
Gallantly through the thickets of old mud.

Tales of your origin I much preferred:
Escaped to sea, I note, from the spring's mesh,
The blood on your bright fingers somehow blurred
When legend, like your element, was fresh.

ditching the gash: throwing waste over a ship's side

I see, beneath the trident, dolphin, crown,
The mermaids bubbling up and down the stair,
Less than a lunatic old killing clown:
Nothing, in fact, of man or god is there.

Yet, folding up these thoughts before the day,
What, with the sea-bell sounding, do I fear?
Whose are those footsteps dragging through the clay,
And whose, ah whose, the loving voice I hear?

JOHN POLRUDDON

JOHN POLRUDDON
All of a sudden
Went out of his house one night,

When a privateer
Came sailing near
Under his window-light.

They saw his jugs
His plates and mugs
His hearth as bright as brass,

His gews and gaws
And kicks and shaws
All through their spying-glass.

They saw his wine
His silver shine
They heard his fiddlers play.

'Tonight,' they said,
'Out of his bed
Polruddon we'll take away.'

And from a skiff
They climbed the cliff
And crossed the salt-wet lawn,

And as they crept
Polruddon slept
The night away to dawn.

'In air or ground
What is that sound?'
Polruddon said, and stirred.

They breathed, 'Be still,
It was the shrill
Of the scritch-owl you heard.'

'O yet again
I hear it plain,
But do I wake or dream?'

'In morning's fog
The otter-dog
Is whistling by the stream.'

'Now from the sea
What comes for me
Beneath my window dark?'

'Lie still, my dear,
All that you hear
Is the red fox's bark.'

Swift from his bed
Polruddon was sped
Before the day was white,

And head and feet
Wrapped in a sheet
They bore him down the height.

And never more
Through his own door
Polruddon went nor came,

Though many a tide
Has turned beside
The cliff that bears his name.

On stone and brick
Was ivy thick,
And the grey roof was thin,

And winter's gale
With fists of hail
Broke all the windows in.

The chimney-crown
It tumbled down
And up grew the green,

Till on the cliff
It was as if
A house had never been.

But when the moon
Swims late or soon
Across St Austell Bay,

What sight, what sound
Haunts air and ground
Where once Polruddon lay?

It is the high
White scritch-owl's cry,
The fox as dark as blood,

And on the hill
The otter still
Whistles beside the flood.

John Polruddon's house was on the cliff over Pentewan, in south Cornwall. The story of his disappearance dates from early Tudor times.

BALAAM

KING BALAK sat on his gaudy throne
His eyes like bits of glass
At the sight of the Children of Is-ra-el
Camped on the river grass.
Hee-haw, said the ass.

Balak called his princes,
Stood them in a silver row.
'Go fetch me a conjuring man,' he said,
'Who will melt them away like snow.'
Said the donkey, *I don't think so.*

Three princes stopped at Balaam's gate,
They tinkled at the bell.
'King Balak bids you curse,' they said,
'The Children of Is-ra-el.'
Said the cuddy, *Just wait a spell.*

Balaam watched and Balaam prayed,
He lifted his head and spoke.
'The Children of Israel must be blessed
For they are God's chosen folk.'
Quite right, said the moke.

Three princes rode to Balak,
Told him what had come to pass.
'I know what I'll do,' King Balak said.
'I'll line his pockets with brass.'
A waste of time, said the ass.

King Balak sent his money-box
But Balaam shook his head.
'Forgive me, brother,' he cried, 'But I
Must listen to the Lord instead.'
Me too, the donkey said.

Early in the morning
  Before the black sun rose,
Jehovah spoke to Balaam,
  Told him to put on his clothes.
    Said the donkey, *The mystery grows!*

'Ride, ride to Moab,'
  The donkey heard Jehovah say,
But before he knew what deed he should do
  Balaam was up and away.
    The cuddy said, *Master, stay!*

They hadn't gone but one mile
  Over river and mire,
When an angel with a burning sword
  Stood as tall as a spire.
    Said the ass, *There's a man on fire!*

Balaam's eyes were heavy,
  His thoughts were as thick as lead
As the donkey galloped off the road
  And into a field of bread,
    Crying, *I spy trouble ahead!*

Balaam beat old Jenny
  Towards the mountain pass,
Didn't see the angel by the grape-yard wall
  Ready with the *coup de grâce.*
    He's here again! said the ass.

Jenny twisted, Jenny turned,
  Knew they were heading for a fall,
Crushed her master's grape-white foot
  Against the vineyard wall.
    Said, *It isn't my fault at all!*

Balaam took his oaken stick,
  Used it with a will.
Can't you see that bird-man? Jenny cried.
  Watch it, or we'll take a spill.
    I think he's aiming to kill!

The donkey carried Balaam
  Under the mountain stack.
When the angel came on for the third time
  She couldn't go fore nor back.
    Said, *This is the end of the track.*

Jenny fell down in the roadway.
  Balaam went over her head.
He saw ten thousand shooting stars.
  'Am I living,' he cried, 'or dead?'
    But the donkey turned and said,

Master, why do you seize your staff
  To tan my hide of grey?
Don't you see that man with the sword in his hand
  Standing in the king's highway?
    He'd have killed us both today.

Balaam opened his silent eyes.
  The angel blazed like a tree.
'Balaam,' he said, 'I would have slain,
  But the donkey would have gone free.'
    Said the ass, *That's news to me.*

'Then I have sinned,' said Balaam,
  'And I must homeward steer.'
'Go forward,' said the angel.
  'Speak God's word, loud and clear.'
    The donkey said, *Hear, hear!*

King Balak stood on the hilltop,
  Israel like sand below.
Balaam lifted up his arms,
  Blessed them where they did go.
    The donkey cried, *Bravo!*

Balaam stood on the mountain,
  Israel was like the sea.
He stretched his hand on the waters
  And blessed what they should be.
    Said the ass, *At last we agree.*

Balaam walked over the mountain,
  The donkey by his side.
He laughed, he wept, he suddenly sneezed.
  'Bless you, my friend,' he cried.
    Bless YOU, the ass replied.

YOUNG EDGCUMBE

YOUNG Edgcumbe spoke by the river,
  Young Edgcumbe spoke by the sea,
'The King with the crown in London town
  Shall never be King to me.

'For he has taken the old King's son
  That is both young and fair,
And wound a prison pillow round
  His head and yellow hair.

'And then he took the other
  That by his brother lay
And with a pin his royal skin
  Of breath has pricked away.

'O never shall young Edgcumbe
  Bow or bend the knee
Or speak or sing "Long live the King"
  To such a man as he.'

But when to London water
  Young Edgcumbe's words were sped,
'He is alive,' the cold King cried,
  'But is already dead!'

Down by the Tamar river
  As young Edgcumbe walked by,
He heard from sleep the woodcock leap
  Into the sudden sky.

As under Cotehele tower
  Young Edgcumbe listening stood,
A branch that broke to Edgcumbe spoke
  Of strangers in the wood.

All under Cotehele tower
  He heard Bodrugan shout,
'Young Edgcumbe yield, for sword and shield
  Ring your good land about!'

But young Edgcumbe was bonny,
  His wits bright as a brand,
And pass and ride on Cotehele side
  He knew as his right hand.

In scarlet-red the sentry
  By the wood-gate did lie,
But redder far the shirt he wore
  When young Edgcumbe passed by.

The King's man for young Edgcumbe
  Lay cold under the hill,
Till Edgcumbe's knife searched out his life
  And left him colder still.

Young Edgcumbe walked by the water,
  Young Edgcumbe walked by the shore,
Bodrugan's steel was at his heel
  And the spring flood before.

Young Edgcumbe took his bonnet
  As he stood on the steep,
And with a stone his cap has thrown
  Into the waters deep.

Light was young Edgcumbe's bonnet,
  Heavy the stone he spun
That struck the swell clear as the bell
  Of Cotehele calling one.

'Alas for poor young Edgcumbe!'
  He heard Bodrugan say.
'For no man from that flood may come
  To fight another day.

'See on the running river
  His cap swims like a snow.
And white as milk, in watered silk
  Young Edgcumbe lies below.

'Farewell, farewell young Edgcumbe,'
  He heard Bodrugan call.
'The river loud it is your shroud
  And the pure sky your pall.

'And now to royal London
  From the far Cornish shore
This message bring unto the King:
  Young Edgcumbe is no more.'

But close as his ten fingers
  And close as hip and thigh,
Young Edgcumbe sees through forest trees
  Bodrugan pass him by.

And when came on the evening
  Young Edgcumbe sailed the Sound,
Nor laid his head on prison bed,
  Nor trod the prison ground.

O when came on the evening
  Young Edgcumbe sailed the sea,
And in the rare and morning air
  Has come to Brittany.

Sound: Plymouth Sound

And with bold Henry Tudor
  Young Edgcumbe spoke as friend,
And freely swore in peace and war
  To serve him to life's end.

Now on the tide to England
  Young Edgcumbe's home again
Where King and crown are both cast down
  On bloody Bosworth plain.

And at the scarlet feast of war
  Men drank the bitter cup,
And one King lay as cold as clay,
  And one there was stood up.

Before the throne of England
  Young Edgcumbe now does stand,
Swears on the ring of England's King
  And kisses his gold hand.

'Young Edgcumbe, Lord of Cotehele,
  Bodrugan's Lord shall be,
His house and land yours to command
  Beside the Cornish sea!'

Across the Bodmin moorland
  Young Edgcumbe's horsemen drum.
Bodrugan fears, Bodrugan hears
  The sounding hoof-beats come.

'I ride,' then cried young Edgcumbe,
'As once you rode for me.
Whom you would slay and was the prey
The hunter now shall be.'

He rode him down the valley,
He rode him up the steep,
Till white as wood Bodrugan stood
Above the Cornish deep.

And from the height, Bodrugan
Sprang down into the swell
That tide on tide at the cliff-side
Hammers a passing-bell.

And ever did the ocean
Under Bodrugan's Leap
With loving care the body fair
Of Lord Bodrugan keep.

And when again to Cotehele
Young Edgcumbe he did ride,
A house of prayer he builded there
Above the water-side.

And still by Cotehele manor
The river-chapel stands,
And at Bodrugan's Leap the deep
Still wrings its watery hands,

Though Edgcumbe and Bodrugan
Long, long they sleep, and sound:
The one his grave in the green wave,
The other in green ground.

Cotehele House, near Calstock, and Bodrugan's Leap, the headland between Mevagissey and the Dodman, are now both National Trust properties in Cornwall.

NELSON GARDENS

As I was walking in Nelson Gardens
A stroppy young seaman came my way,
He put his candid hand in mine
And these were the words I heard him say:

Come with me where the winking waters
Beam as bright as washing-day,
And Old Man Neptune's darling daughters
Round their father's garden play.

Buckle your belt with a Lincoln dollar,
Turn your money and make a wish,
The world will touch your lucky collar,
Jump in your pocket like a flying-fish.

Come with me where the briny billow
Is sweet as the grass upon the hill,
The sun will smooth your single pillow
And the terrible tongue of the clock is still.

Off I went with the easy sailor,
But the truth was hard as stone:
Though we sail the seas together
Each of us must sail alone.

Bitter was the brilliant water,
Ever faster spoke the clock,
And the palace was a prison,
And the pillow was a rock.

Early in the morning when the sun was rising
Up came the moon all rosy-red,
Blew the stars out of the heaven,
Spiked the sky on our masthead.

stroppy: from 'obstropulous'; obstreperous, truculent

By my side I saw my comrade
Freezing in the noonday heat,
And his suit was made of canvas
A lump of lead was at his feet.

Now my hair is white as paper,
Thin my finger as the pen,
As the weather from the winter
Turns to summer once again.

As I was walking in Nelson Gardens
A stroppy young seaman came my way,
He put his candid hand in mine
And those were the words I heard him say.

THE SONG OF SAMUEL SWEET

An incident after the Battle of Sedgemoor, 1685

As I leaned at my window
All in the white of noon,
The sun his silken volleys
Firing at the moon,
Over the dying valley
Slain by the sword of heat,
I heard a horseman riding
And the sound of running feet.

I live in the grassy meadow
Where the little houses lie,
Hoisting their naked chimneys
Like sails upon the sky.
I live where the honey-heather
In a tide comes down the street,
Down to the hurling river,
And my name is Samuel Sweet.

When the cock with crow of silver
Splits as a stone the night,
And over the snoring water
There comes the morning light,
I rise from my strawy pallet
To the leaping light's alarm
And go about my business
Upon my father's farm.

Down in the silent stackyard
  I met the maiden, day,
Her skin as soft as summer
  Her fears all cast away.
And she and I together
  Under the sky did sing,
Till I met by the barnyard
  The soldiers of the King.

From the flowery field of battle
  That blooms all red and white
They had ridden for the rebels
  Through all the steely night.
Far from the field of battle
  That blossoms white and red
There rode three tossing troopers,
  A captain at their head.

'O halt not by my barnyard!
  Ride to the west, away!
No rebel here is hiding
  Among the friendly hay!
Only the wealthy spider
  Building his diamond house,
The bat on the beam, the beetle,
  And the secret harvest-mouse.'

The captain reined and answered
  Beneath the hawthorn tree,
'If a rebel thou art hiding
  We'll hang both him and thee.
By the tongues of my three troopers
  And the springing hawthorn spray
We'll hang you, boy, as surely
  As night relieves the day.

'If a rebel you are hoarding
  Among the golden hay
We'll hang you high as moonlight
  When we ride back this way.
Lighter than any angel,
  Whiter than any dove,
We'll knit a knot of innocence
  With a string as strong as love.'

'Farewell, my bonny captain!
  Farewell, you troopers three!
Seize your sailing standards,
  Never seize you me!
Keep your courage handy,
  Keep your justice dry,
You will never like a banner
  Hang me from the sky!'

I watched them as they galloped
  Down the leaf-hung lane,
The hooves beating a warning
  Over the wheeling plain.
I climbed the leaning ladder
  And in the brittle hay,
His face as pale as morning,
  A wounded soldier lay.

He wore no scarlet jacket
  Nor shirt of linen fine,
He wore no silver buckles
  Nor campaign medals nine.
He wore no lace at his pocket
  Nor of diamond spurs the best,
Only the badge of battle
  Pinned to his bleeding breast.

I watched his slow surrender
  To the daggers of the hay,
The blood that from his body
  Poured like wine away.
I saw death smile and enter
  Trailing his coat so smart,
On sentry-go to plunder
  The jewel of the heart.

'Goodbye, goodbye, dear father
  Whom I did never meet,
And goodbye now to mother
  Who lives on easy street.
I was not meant for a soldier,
  I do not want to die,
But I must take a journey
  Across the silver sky.

'Part my hair in the middle,
  Put a clean shirt on my back!
Hark, I hear the bugle
  And the mourning muskets' crack!
Cover me with a banner,
  Ring the funeral bell!
But first, O comrade, fetch me
  Some water from the well.'

I could not give a pillow
  Nor comb his hair so fine,
I had no shirt of linen,
  Nor cruse of oil and wine.
But as I fetched the water
  From the dazzling spring
I saw within the barnyard
  The soldiers of the King.

'O captain, but I knew not
  Dying among the hay
When you rode by at sunrise
  A rebel soldier lay.
Speak, and he will answer!
  Stand in your stirrup, call!
Ere death shall freeze his fingers
  And silent spread its shawl.'

The mirror of the morning,
  Broken by troopers three,
Flashed its brilliant warning—
  But never a word spoke he.
Never a word he answered
  From his yellow bed,
Lying asleep for ever
  In the bivouac of the dead.

'Rig the gallows, troopers!
  Make the ship shine!
Here's a likely cabin-boy
  For the death or glory line!
Give him a hempen collar
  As he heavenward steers,
The clouds about his ankles,
  The stars about his ears.'

'O captain, do not hang me
  From the mast so high,
Nor stand me like a trooper
  In the barrack of the sky.
Hang me not for a rebel,
  Nor fire the fatal gun,
I was not made for a hero,
  I was made to run.

'Faster than the storm-bird
  Beating up the west,
Swifter than the serpent
  In the sea's breast,
Lighter than the lariat
  Falling from the sun,
Faster than fear,
  My captain, I run!'

'Cut him down, troopers,
  From the forest skies,
Break away the bandage
  That binds his clear eyes.
Let him go a-coursing
  My charger and me!
If he be the victor
  He shall go free!

'If he flies faster
  Than the sea-foam,
Faster than my war-horse,
  He shall fly home.
As I ride over
  The valley's open knife,
If the boy pass me:
  He shall have his life!'

'Where the glass river
  Runs his sword through
The green breast of the valley,
  I am running too!
Lend me your wings, eagle!
  Strong winds, your breath!
That I may race the rider
  And his drummer, death.'

'As the happy hunter
  Aims the accurate gun,
As the raving rifleman
  Knows the battle's won,
Come away, charger,
  With your hooves fleet!
If we win or if we lose
  The prize is Samuel Sweet!'

'O captain, I am waiting
  By the empty tree
As your horse of fire
  Comes blazing on the lea.
See, my feet are bloody,
  With salt my eyes are blind
For captain, I have left you
  Far, far behind.

'Why do you frown, captain,
  As I bend the knee,
Nor tell your tossing troopers
  That I may go free?
Why do you tie my collar
  With a shining strand,
Nor send me home to mother,
  A ring-dove in my hand?'

'Launch the gallows, hangman,
  On the bay of heaven.
Take aboard a passenger
  And his sins all seven.
Pull him up the rigging
  As high as he will fly,
A captain's request-man
  In the sessions of the sky.'

'Lord, the drunken gibbet
  Steering in the clouds
With his wooden fingers
  Wraps me in his shrouds.
Murdered by my captain,
  Murdered by my King,
Murdered by the water
  From the weeping spring.

'Murdered by the rebel
  In the reeking hay,
Murdered by the bragging night
  Who has ransomed day.
When the shepherd, morning,
  Shoots his golden sling,
Listen to the warning
  And the song I sing:

'When the gangs of battle
  Press all through the day,
The innocent and guilty
  Are stolen all away.
Fire the starting pistol,
  Fire a parting prayer
For I run for ever
  In the alleys of the air.'

As I leaned at my window
  All in the white of noon,
The sun his silken volleys
  Firing at the moon,
Over the dying valley
  Slain by the sword of heat,
I heard a horseman riding
  And the sound of running feet.

ST MARTHA AND THE DRAGON

I

IN FAR Provence, where runs the brawny river
Its pride of waters to the southern sea,
And where, on lion-coloured hill and valley
There stand the cypress and the olive tree,
Under a lighted sky of spreading silver
The farmer moves, a priest within his shrine,
To tend the candles of the fig and orange,
And sprinkle his last-planted stock with wine.

But where, by ancient Tarascon, the water
Still breasts the plain, a curse once dried the air,
And every fruit on every tree was withered,
And of its riches all the land was bare.
For, by a wood of black and naked thickets,
Of river-grit, and serpent-haunted stones,
With screeching breath and burning tongue, a dragon
Dwelt in a den of newly gathered bones.

Shepherd and sheep were slaughtered in the meadow,
Slain was the fox that flickered on the hill,
The ox, once garlanded, lay in the furrow,
Smashed was the plough, silent the creaking mill.
Torn was the otter from its house of water,
Birds from the sky, and from the stream the swan,
And still the dragon issued forth unvanquished,
And the great engines of its breath fumed on.

And when of land the monster had grown weary
Beneath the weedy waters it would go,
And rising, seize the fisher, boat and boatman,
Drag them in green and dripping jaws below.
Sharp were the sorrows of that wounded country
For all its dead, and all its dreadful fame,
While from the grieving world a hundred heroes
With sword and lance and rippling pennant came.

But none returned to tell a famous story
Of how the dragon died, and of the fight.
Only in broken blood and bone were written
Their histories in letters red and white.
With fasting, prayer and sacrifice, the people
Addressed their stone-faced gods, their sins forswore,
Till out of the unknown, with cross for mainmast,
A boat pierced the horizon, made for shore.

That sea-country, a good and gentle mother,
Softly received the vessel at its side,
As from the deck three sailor saints came walking
And praising God among the yellow tide:
Grave Lazarus, who walked home from his funeral,
Mary, with spikenard for God's own feet,
And Martha, who with cooking-pot for psalter
And brooms for prayers kept home, like heaven, sweet.

The saints three from the Middle Sea delivered
Knelt down beside the bay, to God gave praise;
Fondly embraced, bade farewell to each other,
And, armed with faith, went their appointed ways.
Eastward strode Lazarus, and westward Mary,
Under the falling colours of the sun,
While Martha, taking up her stick and bundle,
Turned face and fortune north to Tarascon.

Slowly she walked her way beside the river,
Her hair she wore with neither braid nor pin,
A cloak of purple linen at her shoulder,
Her turban of the whitest camel-skin.
And when the young light on the hill came springing
And as she journeyed onward with the day
This was the song she never tired of singing,
And these the words that she was heard to say:

II

'My home is in Bethany,
  Martha my name,
When my Master He died
  To Provence I came
In a boat with no rudder
  Nor paddle nor sail,
With never a zephyr
  And never a gale.

'And when on the sea-shore
  I walked up the strand,
There came a Town Captain
  With gold in his hand.
"O Martha, Saint Martha,"
  He cried as he stood,
"Save us from the dragon
  Within the Black Wood!

' "It's head is a tiger's,
  A lion's its jaw,
On six human feet
  Are nailed the bear's claw.
As strong as a jail
  Are the spikes on its shell,
Its tail a stout timber
  No woodman can fell.

' "With the mane of a horse
  And the frame of a bull,
Its teeth, swords and daggers
  That no man can pull,
It swims in the fresh
  And it swims in the brine
As landsmen and watermen,
  Martha, know fine.

' "And many a traveller
Who sailed by our shore
Fell down the steep water
To rise up no more;
And many a soldier
Of many a fame
Rode out to the Black Wood
But home never came.

' "Ungathered our harvest,
Our barns they are bare.
No man to the farm
Or the field may repair.
All swallowed our flocks
And our hope it is gone.
For food to our children
We give but a stone.

' "The temple fires burn
But no word the gods say,
Our sacrifice turning
To dust and to clay.
O Martha, good Martha,"
The Captain did cry,
"From the dragon deliver
Us all, or we die!" '

III

St Martha, pausing in her onward path,
Reflected,
'My aid is less than nothing, save by God
Directed.'

'God?' cried the Captain. 'To which god do you
Your prayers advance?
Mere words are useless in this case without
A sword or lance.'

'Captain,' replied the Saint, 'your argument
I must reject.
The force of arms has so far proved, it seems,
To no effect.'

'What else,' the Captain said, 'in evil's face
May then be moved?
Strength must be met by strength. Through ceaseless
  time
This is long proved.'

'The spirit,' said the Saint, 'that down from heaven
Came as the dove
At Jordan-side; the symbol and the sign
Of perfect love.'

Thus did they say, and through the droning day
They journeyed on,
Till like a pall hung down the broken wall
Of Tarascon.

IV

The watchman opened the city gate.
He passed them through, he closed it strait.
Fear like a moth flew round the town
As the night came up and the sun went down.

No sound from the tavern, no spitting drum.
The windows were blind, the doors were dumb.
About their houses the people crept.
With sonorous snores the dragon slept.

The Captain stopped by a tavern-side,
A tarry door he opened wide.
'Take linen and water and wine and bread
For body and soul, good Saint,' he said.

'A light of rushes, a curtain neat,
A pallet of straw both pure and sweet,
That armed with God's own strength you rise
When the dragon jumps out of the morning skies.'

And wrapped in his cloak, the Captain tall
Watched for the dawn by the eastern wall,
While Martha knelt and Martha prayed
That the God of Gods should lend His aid.

Martha whispered her holy words
That help should come from the Lord of Lords,
And many a prayer she spoke as she lay
Till the black of the night had turned to grey.

V

St Martha she neither slept nor woke
But rested safe and rested sure,
Until a storm of voices broke
As though the beast's before her door.

Then she, with faith her sword and shield
Stepped out with prayer and stepped with praise
With never a fear of danger near
Or what dread sight might meet her gaze.

VI

No dragon nor monster
Stood there in the light,
But the people to arm
The brave Saint for the fight.

There was one with a broadsword
And one with a pike,
There was one with a pole-axe
And one with a spike.

One carried a falchion,
Another a glaive,
There was one with a broomstick
And one with a stave.

There was one with a catapult,
One with a mask,
And one with a cleaver
And one with a casque.

There was one with a mattock
And one with a thong,
One with a paddle
And one with a prong.

There was truncheon and bludgeon
And cudgel and bill,
And the beam and the tackle
Brought up from the mill.

There was cudgel and quarter-staff,
Hammer and hoe,
Javelin, battle-axe,
Arrow and bow.

And as the good people
Saint Martha did view,
Around her white feet
All their weapons they threw.

She stood there as still
As the stem of an oak,
And these were the words
To the people she spoke:

VII

'No weapon at my hand or side
Of iron or of steel
Will serve to bring the dragon down
And all your sorrows heal.

'So take the weapon from my hand,
The armour from my breast,
And take away the golden helm
And take away the crest.

'And take the gloves, and take the greaves
That lock me to the land,
That free of iron and of steel
Before my fate I stand.'

VIII

'Dear people all
  Who live in thrall,'
    She said,
      'Pray do not grieve.

'For pure and whole
  Shall be the soul
    Of him who will believe.

'Armed but with love
  By God above
    To the Black Wood I go,

'That from your night
  You turn to light,
    And His great mercy know.'

IX

But O the people wept,
And O the people cried
To see the Saint
With no sword at her side.

As big as a cloud
They sighed with one breath
To see St Martha
Walk to her death.

They climbed up the trees
As high as they could
To see St Martha
Walk to the wood.

They saw her pour
In a silver shell
The water sweet
From the Black Wood well.

'Come back, Martha!'
She heard them call
As she walked away
From the high town wall.

Till all down the valley
And under the hill
The wide earth trembled,
And the Saint stood still.

And on her lips
Was the good Lord's name
As with fire and fury
The
dragon
came.

X

Out of the broken wood the dragon thundered
Unseeing, as the Saint gazed calmly on,
While black upon the canvas sky behind her
The citizens looked down from Tarascon.
And here and there, through whirling land and water,
With rapid tusk and claw the monster thrust,
Ran, easy as a crocodile, the river,
Swam like a lizard through the desert dust.

The scars it bore of many a bitter combat
Like battle-honours shone on every scale
As now it smeared its jaws in the burned branches
And snapped an oak-tree with its beamy tail.
Then of its game the dragon seemed to weary
And slithered, listless, to the waterside,
Lay as if shipwrecked in the gleaming shallows
And floated out its tongue upon the tide.

And, staring in the green glass of the river,
It saw reflected at its brazen flank
The gentle Saint, alone, unarmed, and standing
Above its smoking head upon the bank.
With flames for eyes and voice of the volcano
It scaled with six and thirty claws the hill,
Springing its trap of jaws where good St Martha
Stood in its blast of breath, serene and still.

Silence like snow upon the plain descended.
It seemed as if the river ceased to run.
No voice was heard, no bird moved in the thicket
As the beast rose and blotted out the sun.
And to the citizens then spoke St Martha
As round and ever round the dragon stole.
'If you are ready to believe, good people,
All things are possible for heart and soul.'

XI

'Any brute, any bully,'
  They heard the Saint say,
'With a little good fortune
  A dragon may slay.

'With sword or with buckler,
  With spear or with bow,
Any villain or hero
  May lay a beast low.

'With bettle or chisel,
  A sling or a pin,
You may kill a bold dragon—
  But killing's a sin.

'And blessed is he
  That dread evil will move
With the weapons of faith
  And the power of love!'

XII

So the dragon it watched
  With a red and yellow eye
To see the kind of trick
  St Martha would try.

The dragon it waited,
  Cocked its golden head,
Wondered when St Martha
  Would try and strike it dead.

It rattled all its golden scales,
  Rehearsed each golden claw,
Worried at the summer air
  With a golden jaw.

bettle: a type of mallet. A bettle and chisel are used for splitting slate

XIII

And with a silver sprinkler
  Held in her hand
St Martha she walked
  On the shaking land.

But though the dragon raged,
  And though the dragon roared,
St Martha walked on
  In the name of the Lord.

The people watched it flame,
  The people watched it flare,
But St Martha never turned
  Her head or hair.

The dragon's mouth it opened
  And its eyes went boss,
As she wrote on the air
  The sign of the Cross.

She wrote for the dragon
  A cross on the sky,
And it blinked and it blundered
  And
            thundered,
                        'Why?'

XIV

'I do not come, good beast,' then said St Martha,
'To spill your blood or crack your golden spine.
Your life I crave not, and it is my prayer,
Dear monster, that you do not crave for mine.
All things are possible, and with your blessing . . . '
'Mine?' the beast roared. '*Yours*,' she said, 'I shall prove
How, without sword or buckler, I may win you
From evil by the power of human love.'

As if becalmed by gentleness, the monster
Stopped in mid-screech, suddenly dropped a jaw,
Amazed that Martha should not shake nor shudder,
But stand undaunted by its tooth and claw.
Then, sprinkling its brow with holy water,
She cast her belt of horse-hair round its head,
And all the citizens they watched and wondered
As to the riverside the beast she led.

'I do not come, good beast,' again said Martha,
'With your black blood these fields and farms to drown.
I have no trick or magic charm to bring you
In fifty separate pieces to the town.
Only repent,' (she wagged a holy finger)
'Of all your crimes. Repent to the heart's core
That God's great gust of love your brow unfurrows
Smooth as the sand upon the river shore.'

And from the dragon's reeking throat St Martha
Her belt of horse-hair loosened and untied,
And spoke, though never a word she said, of mercy
As with her linen cloak its wounds she dried.
One hand she rested on its giant shoulder
And one upon a claw, in loving trust,
Till from the dragon's eye, big as a boulder
A tear thumped down upon the desert dust.

'Swim to the healing sea, as does to heaven
The wounded soul that but for love had died,
For all your sins are freely now forgiven!'
'Amen! Amen!' the watching people cried.
And bowing down its head, the tender dragon
Of all its thousand sins repented sore,
Plunged like an otter in the sounding river
And on the ravaged plain was seen no more.

St Martha raised her hands in proud thanksgiving.
'Observe,' to all the citizens she said,
'How, like a tree, love grows to its green summer
Where cruel hate and envy once had bred!'
And all the earth, as from a deathly slumber,
Glittered with sudden leaves and flowers sweet;
The vines unfurled their standards, and the valley
Filled with a winding flood of harvest wheat.

From Saint and dragon having learned God's story
Of love and mercy, by the river fair
The people built a cabin for St Martha
Where once the flowering land was dark and bare.
And always at her hearth and home, St Martha
Kept for both humble rich and poor a place;
And here in holy joy she lived and laboured
Until at last to heaven she turned her face.

And when the Gates of Paradise she entered
There stood Lord Jesus in the light divine.
'As in your house,' He said, 'you have received me
I now receive you, blessed Saint, in mine.'
And homewards, through the deepest deep, the dragon
Swam to the silence of the ocean floor,
And close above its head the toiling water
Drew its dark net of tides for evermore.

The figure of the dragon of Tarascon (the Tarasque) is still paraded round the town, twice a year: on the Thursday after Trinity Sunday, and on St Martha's Day, 29 July. On the first occasion he acts very fiercely; on the second, he is quiet and well behaved.

EAGLE ONE, EAGLE TWO

EAGLE ONE, eagle two,
  Standing on the wall,
Your wings a-spread are made of lead,
  You never fly at all.

High on the roof, Britannia
  Holds her fishing-prong,
And she and they as white as clay
  Stand still the whole day long.

And one looks to the eastward,
  One to the setting sun,
And one looks down upon the town
  Until the day is done.

But when the Quarterjacks their twelve
  Upon the black town beat,
And when the moon's a gold balloon
  Blowing down Castle Street,

Then with her spear, Britannia
  The eagles both will guide
To drink their fill under the hill
  Down by the riverside.

And when the Town Hall Quarterjacks
  The hour of one beat plain,
Eagles and queen may all be seen
  On wall and roof again.

But now I am a grown man
  And hear the midnight bell,
Ask, is it true, the tale I knew
  That still the children tell?

I only know at midnight
   Softly I go by,
Nor look at all on roof and wall.
   Do not ask me why.

RILEY

DOWN in the water-meadows Riley
Spread his wash on the bramble-thorn,
Sat, one foot in the moving water,
Bare as the day that he was born.

Candid was his curling whisker,
Brown his body as an old tree-limb,
Blue his eye as the jay above him
Watching him watch the minjies swim.

Four stout sticks for walls had Riley,
His roof was a rusty piece of tin,
As snug in the lew of a Cornish hedgerow
He watched the seasons out and in.

He paid no rates, he paid no taxes,
His lamp was the moon hung in the tree.
Though many an ache and pain had Riley
He envied neither you nor me.

Many a friend from bush or burrow
To Riley's hand would run or fly,
And soft he'd sing and sweet he'd whistle
Whatever the weather in the sky,

Till one winter's morning Riley
From the meadow vanished clean.
Gone was the rusty tin, the timber,
As if old Riley had never been.

minjies: small minnows
lew: lee

What strange secret had old Riley?
Where did he come from? Where did he go?
Why was his heart as light as summer?
Never know now, said the jay. *Never know*.

I SAW A JOLLY HUNTER

I SAW a jolly hunter
  With a jolly gun
Walking in the country
  In the jolly sun.

In the jolly meadow
  Sat a jolly hare.
Saw the jolly hunter.
  Took jolly care.

Hunter jolly eager—
  Sight of jolly prey.
Forgot gun pointing
  Wrong jolly way.

Jolly hunter jolly head
  Over heels gone.
Jolly old safety catch
  Not jolly on.

Bang went the jolly gun.
  Hunter jolly dead.
Jolly hare got clean away.
  Jolly good, I said.

WHAT HAS HAPPENED TO LULU?

WHAT HAS happened to Lulu, mother?
  What has happened to Lu?
There's nothing in her bed but an old rag doll
  And by its side a shoe.

Why is her window wide, mother,
  The curtain flapping free,
And only a circle on the dusty shelf
  Where her money-box used to be?

Why do you turn your head, mother,
  And why do the tear-drops fall?
And why do you crumple that note on the fire
  And say it is nothing at all?

I woke to voices late last night,
  I heard an engine roar.
Why do you tell me the things I heard
  Were a dream and nothing more?

I heard somebody cry, mother,
  In anger or in pain,
But now I ask you why, mother,
  You say it was a gust of rain.

Why do you wander about as though
  You don't know what to do?
What has happened to Lulu, mother?
  What has happened to Lu?

IF YOU SHOULD GO TO CAISTOR TOWN

IF YOU should go to Caistor town
  Where my true love has gone,
Ask her why she went away
  And left me here alone.

She said the Caistor sky was blue,
  The wind was never cold,
The pavements were all made of pearl,
  The young were never old.

Never a word she told me more
  But when the year was fled,
Upon a bed of brightest earth
  She laid her gentle head.

When I went up to Caistor
  My suit was made of black,
And all her words like summer birds
  Upon the air came back.

O when I went to Caistor
  With ice the sky was sown,
And all the streets were chill and grey
  And they were made of stone.

TELL ME, TELL ME, SARAH JANE

TELL ME, tell me, Sarah Jane,
  Tell me, dearest daughter,
Why are you holding in your hand
  A thimbleful of water?
Why do you hold it to your eye
  And gaze both late and soon
From early morning light until
  The rising of the moon?

Mother, I hear the mermaids cry,
  I hear the mermen sing,
And I can see the sailing-ships
  All made of sticks and string.
And I can see the jumping fish,
  The whales that fall and rise
And swim about the waterspout
  That swarms up to the skies.

Tell me, tell me, Sarah Jane,
  Tell your darling mother,
Why do you walk beside the tide
  As though you loved none other?
Why do you listen to a shell
  And watch the billows curl,
And throw away your diamond ring
  And wear instead the pearl?

Mother I hear the water
  Beneath the headland pinned,
And I can see the seagull
  Sliding down the wind.
I taste the salt upon my tongue
  As sweet as sweet can be.

Tell me, my dear, whose voice you hear?

  It is the sea, the sea.

AT CANDLEMAS

'If Candlemas be fine and clear
There'll be two winters in that year';

But all the day the drumming sun
Brazened it out that spring had come,

And the tall elder on the scene
Unfolded the first leaves of green.

But when another morning came
With frost, as Candlemas with flame,

The sky was steel, there was no sun,
The elder leaves were dead and gone.

Out of a cold and crusted eye
The stiff pond stared up at the sky,

And on the scarcely breathing earth
A killing wind fell from the north;

But still within the elder tree
The strong sap rose, though none could see.

TOM BONE

MY NAME is Tom Bone,
I live all alone
In a deep house on Winter Street.
  Through my mud wall
  The wolf-spiders crawl
  And the mole has his beat.

On my roof of green grass
All the day footsteps pass
In the heat and the cold,
  As snug in a bed
  With my name at its head
  One great secret I hold.

Tom Bone, when the owls rise
In the drifting night skies
Do you walk round about?
  All the solemn hours through
  I lie down just like you
  And sleep the night out.

Tom Bone, as you lie there
On your pillow of hair,
What grave thoughts do you keep?
  Tom says, 'Nonsense and stuff!
  You'll know soon enough.
  Sleep, darling, sleep.'

MY YOUNG MAN'S A CORNISHMAN

MY YOUNG man's a Cornishman
  He lives in Camborne town,
I met him going up the hill
  As I was coming down.

His eye is bright as Dolcoath tin,
  His body as china clay,
His hair is dark as Werrington Wood
  Upon St Thomas's Day.

He plays the rugby football game
  On Saturday afternoon,
And we shall walk on Wilsey Down
  Under the bouncing moon.

My young man's a Cornishman,
  Won't leave me in the lurch,
And one day we shall married be
  Up to Trura church.

He's bought me a ring of Cornish gold,
  A belt of copper made,
At Bodmin Fair for my wedding-dress
  A purse of silver paid.

And I shall give him scalded cream
  And starry-gazy pie,
And make him a saffron cake for tea
  And a pasty for by and by.

My young man's a Cornishman,
  A proper young man is he,
And a Cornish man with a Cornish maid
  Is how it belongs to be.

Trura church: Truro Cathedral
starry-gazy pie: fish pie, made of pilchards. The fish are cooked whole, with the heads piercing the crust as though gazing up to the heavens.

LOGS OF WOOD

WHEN IN the summer sky the sun
Hung like a golden ball,
John Willy from the workhouse came
And loudly he would bawl:

Wood! Wood! Logs of wood
To keep out the cold!
Shan't be round tomorrow!
They all must be sold!

But O the sky was shining blue
And green was the spray.
It seemed as if the easy days
Would never pass away.

And when John Willy came to town
The laughter it would start,
And we would smile as he went by
Pushing his wooden cart.

John Willy, I can see you still,
Coming down Tower Street,
Your pointed nose, your cast-off clothes,
Your Charlie Chaplin feet.

And like the prophet you would stand
Calling loud and long,
But there were few who listened to
The story of your song.

Wood! Wood! Logs of wood
To keep out the cold!
Shan't be round tomorrow!
They all must be sold!

But now the snow is on the hill,
  The ice is on the plain,
And dark as dark a shadow falls
  Across my window-pane.

Tomorrow, ah, tomorrow—
  That name I did not fear
Until Tomorrow came and said,
  Good morrow. I am here.

LORD LOVELACE

LORD LOVELACE rode home from the wars,
  His wounds were black as ice,
While overhead the winter sun
  Hung out its pale device.

The lance was tattered in his hand,
  Sundered his axe and blade,
And in a bloody coat of war
  Lord Lovelace was arrayed.

And he was sick and he was sore
  But never sad was he,
And whistled bright as any bird
  Upon an April tree.

'Soon, soon,' he cried, 'at Lovelace Hall
  Fair Ellen I shall greet,
And she with loving heart and hand
  Will make my sharp wounds sweet.

'And Young Jehan the serving-man
  Will bring the wine and bread,
And with a yellow link will light
  Us to the bridal bed.'

But when he got to Lovelace Hall
  Burned were both wall and stack,
And in the stinking moat the tower
  Had tumbled on its back.

And none welcomed Lord Lovelace home
  Within the castle shell,
And ravaged was the land about
  That Lord Lovelace knew well.

Long in his stirrups Lovelace stood
  Before his broken door,
And slowly rode he down the hill
  Back to the bitter war.

Nor mercy showed he from that day,
  Nor tear fell from his eye,
And rich and poor both fearful were
  When Black Lovelace rode by.

This tale is true that now I tell
  To woman and to man,
As Fair Ellen is my wife's name
  And mine is Young Jehan.

MILLER'S END

WHEN WE moved to Miller's End,
  Every afternoon at four
A thin shadow of a shade
  Quavered through the garden-door.

Dressed in black from top to toe
  And a veil about her head
To us all it seemed as though
  She came walking from the dead.

With a basket on her arm
  Through the hedge-gap she would pass,
Never a mark that we could spy
  On the flagstones or the grass.

When we told the garden-boy
  How we saw the phantom glide,
With a grin his face was bright
  As the pool he stood beside.

'That's no ghost-walk,' Billy said,
  'Nor a ghost you fear to stop—
Only old Miss Wickerby
  On a short cut to the shop.'

So next day we lay in wait,
  Passed a civil time of day,
Said how pleased we were she came
  Daily down our garden-way.

Suddenly her cheek it paled,
  Turned, as quick, from ice to flame.
'Tell me,' said Miss Wickerby.
  'Who spoke of me, and my name?'

'Bill the garden-boy.'

She sighed,

Said, 'Of course, you could not know
How he drowned—that very pool—
A frozen winter—long ago.'

MARY, MARY MAGDALENE

On the south wall of the church of St Mary Magdalene at Launceston in Cornwall is a granite figure of the saint. The children of the town say that a stone lodged on her back will bring good luck.

MARY, Mary Magdalene
Lying on the wall,
I throw a pebble on your back.
Will it lie or fall?

Send me down for Christmas
Some stockings and some hose,
And send before the winter's end
A brand-new suit of clothes.

Mary, Mary Magdalene
Under a stony tree,
I throw a pebble on your back.
What will you send me?

I'll send you for your christening
A woollen robe to wear,
A shiny cup from which to sup,
And a name to bear.

Mary, Mary Magdalene
Lying cool as snow,
What will you be sending me
When to school I go?

I'll send a pencil and a pen
That write both clean and neat,
And I'll send to the schoolmaster
A tongue that's kind and sweet.

Mary, Mary Magdalene
Lying in the sun,
What will you be sending me
Now I'm twenty-one?

I'll send you down a locket
As silver as your skin,
And I'll send you a lover
To fit a gold key in.

Mary, Mary Magdalene
Underneath the spray,
What will you be sending me
On my wedding-day?

I'll send you down some blossom,
Some ribbons and some lace,
And for the bride a veil to hide
The blushes on her face.

Mary, Mary Magdalene
Whiter than the swan,
Tell me what you'll send me,
Now my good man's dead and gone.

I'll send to you a single bed
On which you must lie,
And pillows bright where tears may light
That fall from your eye.

Mary, Mary Magdalene
Now nine months are done,
What will you be sending me
For my little son?

I'll send you for your baby
A lucky stone, and small,
To throw to Mary Magdalene
Lying on the wall.

MY MOTHER SAW A DANCING BEAR

MY MOTHER saw a dancing bear
By the schoolyard, a day in June.
The keeper stood with chain and bar
And whistle-pipe, and played a tune.

And bruin lifted up its head
And lifted up its dusty feet,
And all the children laughed to see
It caper in the summer heat.

They watched as for the Queen it died.
They watched it march. They watched it halt.
They heard the keeper as he cried,
'Now, roly-poly!' 'Somersault!'

And then, my mother said, there came
The keeper with a begging-cup,
The bear with burning coat of fur,
Shaming the laughter to a stop.

They paid a penny for the dance,
But what they saw was not the show;
Only, in bruin's aching eyes,
Far-distant forests, and the snow.

WHO?

WHO IS that child I see wandering, wandering
Down by the side of the quivering stream?
Why does he seem not to hear, though I call to him?
Where does he come from, and what is his name?

Why do I see him at sunrise and sunset
Taking, in old-fashioned clothes, the same track?
Why, when he walks, does he cast not a shadow
Though the sun rises and falls at his back?

Why does the dust lie so thick on the hedgerow
By the great field where a horse pulls the plough?
Why do I see only meadows, where houses
Stand in a line by the riverside now?

Why does he move like a wraith by the water,
Soft as the thistledown on the breeze blown?
When I draw near him so that I may hear him,
Why does he say that his name is my own?

TEN TYPES OF HOSPITAL VISITOR

I

THE FIRST enters wearing the neon armour
Of virtue.
Ceaselessly firing all-purpose smiles
At everyone present
She destroys hope
In the breasts of the sick,
Who realise instantly
That they are incapable of surmounting
Her ferocious goodwill.

Such courage she displays
In the face of human disaster!

Fortunately, she does not stay long.
After a speedy trip round the ward
In the manner of a nineteen-thirties destroyer
Showing the flag in the Mediterranean,
She returns home for a week
—With luck, longer—
Scorched by the heat of her own worthiness.

II

The second appears, a melancholy splurge
Of theological colours;
Taps heavily about like a healthy vulture
Distributing deep-frozen hope.

The patients gaze at him cautiously.
Most of them, as yet uncertain of the realities
Of heaven, hell-fire, or eternal emptiness,
Play for safety
By accepting his attentions
With just-concealed apathy,
Except one old man, who cries
With newly sharpened hatred,
'Shove off! Shove off!
'Shove . . . shove . . . shove . . . shove
Off!
Just you
Shove!'

III

The third skilfully deflates his weakly smiling victim
By telling him
How the lobelias are doing,
How many kittens the cat had,
How the slate came off the scullery roof,
And how no one has visited the patient for a
  fortnight
Because everybody
Had colds and feared to bring the jumpy germ
Into hospital.

The patient's eyes
Ice over. He is uninterested
In lobelias, the cat, the slate, the germ.
Flat on his back, drip-fed, his face
The shade of a newly dug-up Pharaoh,
Wearing his skeleton outside his skin,
Yet his wits as bright as a lighted candle,
He is concerned only with the here, the now,
And requires to speak
Of nothing but his present predicament.

It is not permitted.

IV

The fourth attempts to cheer
His aged mother with light jokes
Menacing as shell-splinters.
'They'll soon have you jumping round
Like a gazelle,' he says.
'Playing in the football team.'
Quite undeterred by the sight of kilos
Of plaster, chains, lifting-gear,
A pair of lethally designed crutches,
'You'll be leap-frogging soon,' he says.
'Swimming ten lengths of the baths.'

At these unlikely prophecies
The old lady stares fearfully
At her sick, sick offspring
Thinking he has lost his reason—

Which, alas, seems to be the case.

V

The fifth, a giant from the fields
With suit smelling of milk and hay,
Shifts uneasily from one bullock foot
To the other, as though to avoid
Settling permanently in the antiseptic landscape.
Occasionally he looses a scared glance
Sideways, as though fearful of what intimacy
He may blunder on, or that the walls
Might suddenly close in on him.

He carries flowers, held lightly in fingers
The size and shape of plantains,
Tenderly kisses his wife's cheek
—The brush of a child's lips—
Then balances, motionless, for thirty minutes
On the thin chair.

At the end of visiting time
He emerges breathless,
Blinking with relief, into the safe light.

He does not appear to notice
The dusk.

VI

The sixth visitor says little,
Breathes reassurance,
Smiles securely.
Carries no black passport of grapes
And visa of chocolate. Has a clutch
Of clean washing.

Unobtrusively stows it
In the locker; searches out more.
Talks quietly to the Sister
Out of sight, out of earshot, of the patient.
Arrives punctually as a tide.
Does not stay the whole hour.

Even when she has gone
The patient seems to sense her there:
An upholding
Presence.

VII

The seventh visitor
Smells of bar-room after-shave.
Often finds his friend
Sound asleep: whether real or feigned
Is never determined.

He does not mind; prowls the ward
In search of second-class, lost-face patients
With no visitors
And who are pretending to doze
Or read paperbacks.

He probes relentlessly the nature
Of each complaint, and is swift with such
Dilutions of confidence as,
'Ah! You'll be worse
Before you're better.'

Five minutes before the bell punctuates
Visiting time, his friend opens an alarm-clock
  eye.
The visitor checks his watch.
Market day. The Duck and Pheasant will be still
  open.

Courage must be refuelled.

VIII

The eighth visitor looks infinitely
More decayed, ill and infirm than any patient.
His face is an expensive grey.
He peers about with antediluvian eyes
As though from the other end
Of time.
He appears to have risen from the grave
To make this appearance.
There is a whiff of white flowers about him;
The crumpled look of a slightly used shroud.
Slowly he passes the patient
A bag of bullet-proof
Home-made biscuits,
A strong, death-dealing cake—
'To have with your tea,'
Or a bowl of fruit so weighty
It threatens to break
His glass fingers.

The patient, encouraged beyond measure,
Thanks him with enthusiasm, not for
The oranges, the biscuits, the cake,
But for the healing sight
Of someone patently worse
Than himself. He rounds the crisis-corner;
Begins a recovery.

IX

The ninth visitor is life.

X

The tenth visitor
Is not usually named.

AT KFAR KANA

THE BUS halts its long brawl
With rock and tar and sun.
The pilgrims trudge to where
The miracle was done:
Each altar the exact
Authenticated site
Of a far, famous act
Which if performed at all
May well have been not here.

I turn away and walk
And watch the pale sun slide,
The furry shadows bloom
Along the hills' rough hide.
Beneath a leafy span
In fast and falling light
Arabs take coffee, scan
The traveller, smoke, talk
As in a dim, blue room.

The distant lake is flame.
Beside the fig's green bell
I lean on a parched bay
Where steps lead to a well.
Two children smile, come up
With water, sharp and bright,
Drawn in a paper cup.
'This place, what is its name?'
'Kfar Kana,' they say,

Gravely resuming free
Pure rituals of play
As pilgrims from each shrine
Come down the dusty way
With ocean-coloured glass,
Embroidered cloths, nun-white,
And sunless bits of brass—
Where children changed for me
Well-water into wine.

ANGEL HILL

A SAILOR came walking down Angel Hill,
He knocked on my door with a right good will,
With a right good will he knocked on my door.
He said, 'My friend, we have met before.'
No, never, said I.

He searched my eye with a sea-blue stare
And he laughed aloud on the Cornish air,
On the Cornish air he laughed aloud
And he said, 'My friend, you have grown too proud.'
No, never, said I.

'In war we swallowed the bitter bread
And drank of the brine,' the sailor said.
'We took of the bread and we tasted the brine
As I bound your wounds and you bound mine.'
No, never, said I.

'By day and night on the diving sea
We whistled to sun and moon,' said he.
'Together we whistled to moon and sun
And vowed our stars should be as one.'
No, never, said I.

'And now,' he said, 'that the war is past
I come to your hearth and home at last.
I come to your home and hearth to share
Whatever fortune waits me there.'
No, never, said I.

'I have no wife nor son,' he said,
'Nor pillow on which to lay my head,
No pillow have I, nor wife nor son,
Till you shall give to me my own.'
No, never, said I.

His eye it flashed like a lightning-dart
And still as a stone then stood my heart.
My heart as a granite stone was still
And he said, 'My friend, but I think you will.'
        No, never, said I.

The sailor smiled and turned in his track
And shifted the bundle on his back
And I heard him sing as he strolled away,
'You'll send and you'll fetch me one fine day.'
        No, never, said I.

SIX WOMEN

SIX WOMEN in a chronic ward, the light
Like dirty water filtering away;
Washed, spruced, and fed, they innocently wear
Their flowered shrouds to face the last of day.

One, flapping endlessly, a landed fish,
Thumps on a beach of sheets. One lies and glares
At her reflection in the ceiling's paint,
Writhes to avoid its gaze, and gabbles prayers.

One, deaf as granite, smiles, begins to speak
To someone she, and she alone, has spied;
Calls from the deep and dewy field her cat,
Holds it, invisible, at her clenched side.

One, crouching, poised as if to pounce, stone-still,
Suddenly gives a start, a little squeak:
A mouse-woman with wild and whitened hair,
Dried flakes of tears like snow cooling her cheek.

One, bird-like, lifting up her blinded head
To sounds beyond the television-blare
Cries out, in a sharp sliver of a voice,
I do not know if anyone is there!

I do not know if anyone is here.
If so, if not so, I must let it be.
I hold your drifted hand; no time to tell
What six dead women hear, or whom they see.

GREEN MAN IN THE GARDEN

GREEN MAN in the garden
  Staring from the tree,
Why do you look so long and hard
  Through the pane at me?

Your eyes are dark as holly,
  Of sycamore your horns,
Your bones are made of elder-branch,
  Your teeth are made of thorns.

Your hat is made of ivy-leaf,
  Of bark your dancing shoes,
And evergreen and green and green
  Your jacket and shirt and trews.

Leave your house and leave your land
  And throw away the key,
And never look behind, he creaked,
  And come and live with me.

I bolted up the window,
  I bolted up the door,
I drew the blind that I should find
  The green man never more.

But when I softly turned the stair
  As I went up to bed,
I saw the green man standing there.
  Sleep well, my friend, he said.

ATHENODORUS

ATHENODORUS, friend, philosopher, sat
Calm as a turnip in this very chair,
Scratched sums on tablets, whispered to his cat,
As goblins streamed by on the howling air.

It was too much for puss. He gave one squall
And left so fast we never saw him go,
Like innocence melted once and for all
Without a trace on the appalling snow.

Unmoved by bat-faced angels drenched with light
The old man wrote for dear life on his slate,
And when a beckoning ghost parted the night
Quietly motioned it to sit and wait.

And how we cheered this rational man! Entranced,
Watched him explain away the bones, the smell,
As, fearless, through the long grass he advanced
Towards the creaking frontier of hell.

Yet, all the time, we knew how it must end,
Heard the loud bang, felt how the palace shook,
Still see the regular ghost, but of my friend
Found only candle, bell, and a burned book.

ON THE BORDER

BY THE window-drizzling leaves,
Underneath the rain's shadow,
'What is that land,' you said, 'beyond
Where the river bends the meadow?

'Is it Cornwall? Is it Devon?
Those promised fields, blue as the vine,
Wavering under new-grown hills;
Are they yours, or mine?'

When day, like a crystal, broke
We saw what we could see.
No Man's Land was no man's land.
It was the sea.

THE FOREST OF TANGLE

DEEP IN in the Forest of Tangle
The King of the Makers sat
With a faggot of stripes for the tiger
And a flitter of wings for the bat.

He'd teeth and he'd claws for the cayman
And barks for the foxes and seals,
He'd a grindstone for sharpening swordfish
And electrical charges for eels.

He'd hundreds of kangaroo-pouches
On bushes and creepers and vines,
He'd hoots for the owls, and for glow-worms
He'd goodness knows how many shines.

He'd bellows for bullfrogs in dozens
And rattles for snakes by the score,
He'd hums for the humming-birds, buzzes for bees,
And elephant trumpets galore.

He'd pectoral fins for sea-fishes
With which they might glide through the air,
He'd porcupine quills and a bevy of bills
And various furs for the bear.

But O the old King of the Makers
With tears could have filled up a bay,
For no one had come to his warehouse
These many long years and a day.

And sadly the King of the Makers
His bits and his pieces he eyed
As he sat on a rock in the midst of his stock
And he cried and he cried and he cried.
He cried and he cried and he cried and he cried,
He cried and he cried and he cried.

HELPSTON

HILLS SANK like green fleets on the land's long rim
About the village of toast-coloured stone.
Leaving the car beside the Blue Bell, we
Walked with a clutch of flowers the clear lane
Towards the grave.

It was well combed, and quiet as before.
An upturned stone boat
Beached at God's thick door.
Only the water in the spiked grave-pot
Smelt sourly of death.
Yet no wind seemed to blow
From off the fen or sea
The flowers flickered in the painted pot
Like green antennae,
As though John Clare from a sounding skull
Brim with a hundred years of dirt and stone
Signalled to us;
And light suddenly breathed
Over the plain.

Later, drinking whisky in the Bull at Peterborough,
The face of the poet
Lying out on the rigid plain
Stared at me
As clearly as it once stared through
The glass coffin-lid
In the church-side pub on his burial day:
Head visible, to prove
The bulging brain was not taken away
By surgeons, digging through the bone and hair
As if to find poems still
Beating there;
Then, like an anchor, to be lowered fast
Out of creation's pain, the stropping wind,
Deep out of sight, into the world's mind.

INFANT SONG

DON'T YOU love my baby, mam,
Lying in his little pram,

Polished all with water clean,
The finest baby ever seen?

Daughter, daughter, if I could
I'd love your baby as I should,

But why the suit of signal red,
The horns that grow out of his head,

Why does he burn with brimstone heat,
Have cloven hooves instead of feet,

Fishing hooks upon each hand,
The keenest tail that's in the land,

Pointed ears and teeth so stark
And eyes that flicker in the dark?

Don't you love my baby, mam?

Dearest, I do not think I can.
I do not, do not think I can.

A LITERARY SCANDAL

WE GOT the old man underground
Stowed safely in a cage profound
With mysteries,
While all around the famous square
The frantic birds rehearsed their air-
Y histories.

The inkpot and the penny pen
Parade the faultless desk as when
The verse took flame,
And guardians of the ticket roll
The deathless avenues patrol
About his name.

Upon this damp, disastrous bed
He laid an indecisive head
As on a tomb,
And from the splendid second wife
He turned and slept away his life:
God knows with whom.

Here, through a skulking, Cornish fog
That politician-tongued old dog
He trotted,
And on this chill and chalky waste
The thousand lapses from good taste
Carefully plotted.

Nothing was more decorous than
The tweed-voiced country gentleman
Not found below,
Discountenancing God, the pack;
Who bore the world upon his back
Into the snow.

But having handed him the palm,
We cannot comprehend the calm
  Dismay
Of one who gazed at good, rough, raw
Creation, hated what he saw
  And walked away.

Patiently, then, the words misread
That from his printed heart now bleed
  Uncancelled, clear,
And loudly on the granite plain
Speak of a passion and a pain
  No one must hear.

LOSS OF AN OIL TANKER

OVER OUR heads the missiles ran
Through skies more desolate than the sea.
In jungles, where man hides from man,
Leaves fell, in springtime, from the tree.

A cracked ship on the Seven Stones lies
Dying in resurrection weather.
With squalid hands we hold our prize:
A drowned fish and a sea-bird's feather.

JACK O' LENT

WHERE ARE you running to, Jack o' Lent,
Your yellow coat so ruined and rent?

I'm going to the sea-shore as fast as I can
To try and find the Galilee man.

What will you have from him, Jack o' Lent,
Before your thirty of silver is spent?

I'll have some fish and I'll have some bread
And some words to cure the pain in my head.

How long will it take you, Jack o' Lent,
Your legs all crooked, your body all bent?

With the help of prayer and the help of praise
It'll take me forty nights and days.

Should you not find him, Jack o' Lent,
What will then be your intent?

I'll find the hungry and find the poor
And scatter my silver at their door.

What will you do then, Jack o' Lent,
If nobody takes a single cent?

I'll go to the rope-maker cunning and old
And buy me a collar against the cold.

Where will your lodging be, Jack o' Lent,
If house and home give no content?

I'll climb as high as heaven's hem
And take my rest on a sycamore stem.

What can we do for you, Jack o' Lent,
If in the fire the tree is pent?

Take the fire and take the flame
And burn the curse from off my name.

What shall we do then, Jack o' Lent,
If all to ashes you are sent?

Take the cinders you can see.
Cross your brow. Remember me.

In Cornwall, figures representing Judas Iscariot, and called 'Jack o' Lent', were once paraded round towns and villages on Ash Wednesday, and were later burnt on bonfires.

A MOMENTARY DEATH

Cecil Day Lewis, 1904–1972

BIRDS FROM sharp branches of the luckless may
Their glittering warnings to the woods relay.
A man must speak when he has words to say.
The poet wrote until his dying day.

For fifty years, across the changing bay
He sailed his patient, scribbled boats away
From a strong tower of breath and country clay.
The poet wrote until his dying day.

His words, like fine leaves, whisper on the spray;
The seasons halt, and do not have their way
Till sifting time tells what will go, will stay
To burn this momentary death away.
The poet wrote until his dying day.

ON BEING ASKED TO WRITE A SCHOOL HYMN

Tune: Buckland
('Loving Shepherd of Thy Sheep')

ON A starless night and still
Underneath a sleeping hill
Comes the cry of sheep and kine
From the slaughter house to mine.

Fearful is the call and near
That I do not want to hear,
Though it has been said by some
That the animal is dumb.

Gone the byre and gone the breeze
And the gently moving trees
As with stabbing eye they run
In a clear, electric sun.

Now, red-fingered to their trade
With the shot and with the blade,
Rubber-booted angels white
Enter as the morning light.

But who wields that knife and gun
Does not strike the blow alone,
And there is no place to stand
Other than at his right hand.

God, who does not dwell on high
In the wide, unwinking sky,
And whose quiet counsels start
Simply from the human heart,

Teach us strong and teach us true
What to say and what to do,
That we love as best we can
All Thy creatures. Even man.

Amen.

LETTER FROM JERICHO

four miles to our east, at a wood palisade, Carolingian
Bavaria stopped, beyond it
unknowable nomads.

—The Cave of Making

AUDEN, today in Jericho,
Standing by the burned wall
Of the gap-tooth town,
I thought I saw you:
A seal up-ended in a loose tweed sack
And carpet-slippers, swaying slightly
In the oven heat, desperately sucking a gasper
As if your last,
And peering with twin volcano eyes
Down a crack in the violent earth
Where the whore's house may have stood
On the rim of the once green city
Under the Mount of Temptation.

Instantly, I forgot the guide,
Buzzing of Joshua's Jericho beneath Tel es-Sultan,
And I was sitting with you by a back-room gas fire
In the Freemasons' Hall
At Edinburgh, that very Scotch September,
While onstage a whiskered American
Detonated a bailiwick of Whitman.

Deadpan, you asked me
(An unrelenting non-gardener)
How my kidney beans were doing that year;
How the children were at school;
Told me your days as a prep-school master
Were among your happiest,
And (you'd just arrived from Kirchstetten)
How necessary it was, in order to aid concentration,
To work in a room with a poor view:
In your case, of Austrian mud and several hectares
Of sugar-beet.

Later, standing in the wings,
I heard you read: no dramatics,
More interested in what you said
Than how you said it;
Airless Stateside vowels
Ricocheting off the kippered panelling
Like custard pies, yet more telling
Than bullets or blood transfusions.

One moment, you were there beside me
In the final line-up, bowing amateurishly,
Modestly retreating crabwise into a corner.
The next, gone: flying back to your home
Four miles from where Carolingian Bavaria stopped—
For all I knew, without benefit of aircraft,
As befits all legitimate companions of Apollo.

'And there,' the guide was saying at Tel es-Sultan,
'The prophet cast on salt, and healed the waters.'

Auden, born public exchanger of winks
At empty solemnities,
For fifty years a seasoner of thought
With seafuls of necessary salt,
Sounding tirelessly against the thumping walls of
cant,
And affirming the civilised virtues
With an unshadowed tongue, meanwhile declaring
The private, shy and loving heart—
I send you this scrape of salt,
This lungful of neat air from Jericho.
Keep healing the waters. Keep station
Till men have need no longer of walls for cities
Or themselves. Above all, help us
To know the nomads.

ZELAH

As I unwound at Zelah Bent
A string of geese to pay the rent
I saw a scaly demon fly
A boulder through the beating sky.

I saw a demon in a cloud,
As the north wind he wailed aloud,
And straight upon the Cornish sand
I saw a silver bowman stand.

I heard a demon in the sky,
I saw a shaft to heaven fly,
And as I went by Zelah Tree
The demon tumbled in the sea.

When I went up to Helston town
They showed me where the stone fell down,
But when I went there yesterday
They told me it had gone away.

I saw no demon in the sky
With other than a secret eye,
And not an angel on the land
Had any but a human hand.

Angel and stone and demon-claw,
These I did see, though never saw.
All these I saw but did not see
As I went down by Zelah Tree
And found beside the fading grass
The sharp, sweet flowers of Michaelmas.

This legend is well known in Cornwall, where St Michael, Archangel (Feast Day, 29 September) is Patron Saint. The stone is said to have fallen in the inn-yard of the Angel at Helston.

WARD 14

TODAY, incredibly, the nurse
Attempts to reason with her—
The mother with the brain three quarters
  struck away

By apoplexy, and other
Assorted fevers and indignities as the body
Slides slowly, O so slowly, to harbour.

'Wake up!' orders the nurse, kindly.
'Open your eyes.'

The mother does so.
'Your son is here,' says the nurse:
A razor-voice stained momentarily with a
  little sugar.

'You mustn't cry
When your son is here.
Mothers don't cry
When their sons are here.
Now be a good girl;
That's a good girl.'

Puzzled, the mother stares at her:
Wonder creasing the face.
'You're going to be a good girl
Now that your son is here
Aren't you?'
'Yes,' says the mother rapidly,
Wide-eyed, astounded.

Her task accomplished, the nurse
Clops purposefully away down the ward
Like a fractious charger
After a small battle.

As soon as she has gone, the mother
Breaks once more into swift, unceasing tears
Of pain, misery, frustration.
The other visitors look at the son
With a compassionate air;
Rather less so at the patient.

Weep on, mother!
It is your right.
It is your due.
Helpless at the foot of your crucifixion
He is not going to deny you that.

THE WHANGBIRD

'Good gracious me,' the whangbird said,
'They told me all your kind were dead.
What brought you back from that cold bed?'
A thread.

'Your face was made of curds and whey,
Your speech was black, your lip was grey.
Something went in your head, they say.'
Away.

'You walked about with quavering tread,
Refused to eat your birthday spread,
Bit on a stone and called it bread.'
Was fed.

'You followed every wind that blows
Through desert salt and seething snows.
What sharpened path was it you chose?'
God knows.

'We can't forget how we were shown
The rough pit where your goods were thrown.
What thought sustained you there alone?'
My own.

'Perhaps your weakness you'd have shed
If only you had gone and wed—
Look at young Harry, look at Fred . . . '
Looking, I said.

And looking at you, dear old thing,
Is that a canker on your wing,
And why do you no longer sing?
Why is your tongue so stale, and why
So limp and lustreless your eye,
And why do you no longer fly?

Furious, the whangbird stopped his spiel
And cried, 'If that's the way you feel—'
A last feather fell from his head.
'Not me! Not me!' he said.
And fled.

ON ALL SOULS' DAY

LAST NIGHT they lit your glass with wine
And brought for you the sweet soul-cake,
And blessed the room with candle-shine
For the grave journey you would make.

They told me not to stir between
The midnight strokes of one and two,
And I should see you come again
To view the scene that once you knew.

'Good night,' they said, and journeyed on.
I turned the key, and—turning—smiled,
And in the quiet house alone
I slept serenely as a child.

Innocent was that sleep, and free,
And when the first of morning shone
I had no need to gaze and see
If crumb, or bead of wine, had gone.

My heart was easy as this bloom
Of waters rising by the bay.
I did not watch where you might come,
For you had never been away.
For you have never been away.

THE ANIMALS' CAROL

Christus natus est! the cock — Christ is born
Carols on the morning dark.

Quando? croaks the raven stiff — When?
Freezing on the broken cliff.

Hoc nocte, replies the crow — This night
Beating high above the snow.

Ubi? Ubi? booms the ox — Where?
From its cavern in the rocks.

Bethlehem, then bleats the sheep — Bethlehem
Huddled on the winter steep.

Quomodo? the brown hare clicks, — How?
Chattering among the sticks.

Humiliter, the careful wren — Humbly
Thrills upon the cold hedge-stone.

Cur? Cur? sounds the coot — Why?
By the iron river-root.

Propter homines, the thrush — For the sake of man
Sings on the sharp holly-bush.

Cui? Cui? rings the chough — To whom?
On the strong, sea-haunted bluff.

Mary! Mary! calls the lamb — Mary
From the quiet of the womb.

Praeterea ex quo? cries — Who else?
The woodpecker to pallid skies.

Joseph, breathes the heavy shire — Joseph
Warming in its own blood-fire.

Ultime ex quo? the owl — Who above all?
Solemnly begins to call.

De Deo, the little stare — Of God
Whistles on the hardening air.

Pridem? Pridem? the jack snipe — Long ago?
From the harsh grass starts to pipe.

Sic et non, answers the fox — Yes and no
Tiptoeing the bitter lough.

Quomodo hoc scire potest? — How do I know this?
Boldly flutes the robin redbreast.

Illo in eandem, squeaks — By going there
The mouse within the barley-sack.

Quae sarcinae? asks the daw — What luggage?
Swaggering from head to claw.

Nulla res, replies the ass, — None
Bearing on its back the Cross.

Quantum pecuniae? shrills — How much money?
The wandering gull about the hills.

Ne nummum quidem, the rook — Not a penny
Caws across the rigid brook.

Nulla resne? barks the dog — Nothing at all?
By the crumbling fire-log.

Nil nisi cor amans, the dove — Only a loving heart
Murmurs from its house of love.

Gloria in Excelsis! Then
Man is God, and God is Man.

SILENT JACK

MY UNCLE Johnnie, known as Silent Jack,
Suffered, despite his name, no special lack
Of words; just kept them growling in his skull,
Jerking their tails, or lying half-awake
Till, without warning, like some starving back-
Yard greyhound one would scud out for the kill
—Frayed flesh, torn fur—or else to chase a joke
Around the bar until it burst, and bled
Under Jack's marble eye. Then dropped down dead.

At Uncle Johnnie's house I'd watch him take
His dinner sitting by the red-tongued grate.
Self-banished, cracking fingers stiff as thorn,
He'd gently breathe a safe and separate air.
Unseen by others, prick my huge, child's stare
With a sharp wink; penal, in socks, and sworn
By pomegranate-faced aunts not to swear,
And then, when the fouled clock struck ten past one,
He and his swag of walling-tools had gone.

I heard his drenched voice waver through the park
An 'Onward, Christian soldiers' at the dark;
Thumps on the black-tarred door. Aunts spiked the way.
'You're frightening the boy.' I hoped he'd stay,
For all the time I knew it was a play.
But, seeing me, he stopped, and turned, and fled,
And when an orchard apple sniped his head,
Thought it a shot; died in the dry field-drain
But resurrected with the day again.

In eighty years he never ventured far
Past the Longstone, but for Lord Kitchener:
Scarecrowed in khaki, kitted out with rum,
Puttees unrolled like Tablets of the Law.
They tried to teach him how to shoot the Hun,
But fighting was an art not Uncle John's.
Came first, they said, in the Retreat from Mons,
And all his country scholarship revived
In bloody situations; and survived.

Though now he's underneath this hump of grass
And named and numbered on the written brass,
I see him slowly wiping tine and blade,
Listening to a hot-cheeked boy who took
Geese not for swans, but ducks. Jack let that pass;
A healing smile. 'It's each man to his trade.'
Six and a half worn words from Silent Jack:
Where all around his drystone speeches stand
Printed across the strong page of the land.

A WEDDING PORTRAIT

YOUNG MAN, young woman, gazing out
Straight-backed, straight-eyed, from what would
  seem
A cloud of sepia and cream,
In your twin pair of eyes I note
A sense of the ridiculous,
Innocent courage, the strange hope
Things might get better in the lean
Year of the *Lusitania*; gas
Used at the Front; Arras and Ypres
More than place-names. 1915.

My father, Driver Causley, stands
Speckless in 2nd Wessex kit,
A riding-crop in ordered hands,
Lanyard well slicked, and buttons lit
With Brasso; military cap
On the fake pillar for an urn.
Khaki roughens his neck. I see
The mouth half-lifted by a scrap
Of smile. It is a shock to learn
How much, at last, he looks like me.

Serene, my mother wears a white
And Sunday look, and at her throat
The vague smudge of a brooch, a mute
Pale wound of coral. The smooth weight
Of hair curves from her brow; gold chain
Circles a wrist to mark the day,
And on the other is the grey
Twist of a bandage for the flame
That tongued her flesh as if to say,
'I am those days that are to come.'

As I walk by them on the stair
A small surprise of sun, a ruse
Of light, gives each a speaking air,
A sudden thrust, though both refuse
—Silent as fish or water-plants—
To break the narrow stream of glass
Dividing us. I was nowhere
That wedding-day, and the pure glance
They shaft me with acknowledges
Nothing of me. I am not here.

The unregarding look appears
To say, somehow, man is a breath,
And at the end hides in the fire,
In bolting water, or the earth.
I am a child again, and move
Sunwards these images of clay,
Listening for their first birth-cry.
And with the breath my parents gave
I warm the cold words with my day:
Will the dead weight to fly. To fly.

SOREL POINT

THE ROCKS, of child's red plasticine,
Blister the sea's strong glass. A pair
Of gulls switchback on curving air.
Thin water yeasts the faultless sand.
Dressed for the day and Sunday-clean
The quarry's hurt, salt-washed and dried,
Spills its neat gut down the cliff-side.
In whitest white and blackest black
The shore-light turns its iron back
On the small sureness where we stand.

Hand on the rail, I lean down to
The almost out of earshot bay;
The taut horizon's silver-grey
Disseverance of blue and blue.
I turn to you, but you are gone
Up the hung path of whitened stone
To where your wife and children wait.
Now dispossessed of the great sea
A stranded tide snakes under me.
Translate, I hear you say. Translate.

SEVEN HOUSES

To David English

THIS IS the house where I was born:
Sepulchre-white, the unsleeping stream
Washing the wall by my child bed.
I shall outlive you all, it said.

This is the house where I was born:
Its eastward pane a rose of light,
A water cross upon my brow
Pointing a path to day from night.

This is the house where I was born:
A spoil of children; and where grew
A bough of words; and printed birds
Awoke, and shook their wings, and flew.

This is the house where I was born:
A dripping mill; a bed of grain;
A voice that said, 'Now you shall know
The gate of blood through which you came.'

This is the house where I was born:
A sea that writhed beneath the floor
And stood upright upon the sands
And beat the door with deep, green hands.

This is the house where I was born:
The silky waters of the bay
A shroud for ships' bones, and a long
Brown garden, dry with insect song.

This is the house where I was born:
Where in the white drifts of the moon
First words, like snowflakes, touched the page
And stayed, unfaded, with the noon.

'Which is the house where I was born?'
I asked the true and turning stream.
That house, the water said, *is known*
Only when life is told and done:

A roof upraised; a stair half-grown,
Willed to the starving rain and sun;
A scuttled wall; a founding-stone;
A house that never was begun.

GRANDMOTHER

RISES before the first bird. Slugs about
In gig-sized slippers. Soothes the anxious whine
Of the washing-machine with small bequests
Collected from our room. Whacks up the blind.
Restores a lost blanket. Firmly ignores,
With total grace, your nakedness. And mine.

At seven the kitchen's a lit quarter-deck.
She guillotines salami with a hand
Veined like Silesia. Deals black, damp bread,
Ingots of butter, cheese, eggs grenade-strong.
Thinks, loudly, in ground German. Sends a long
And morning glance across anonymous crops
To where the *autobahn*, fluent with cars,
Spools north to Frankfurt, and unpromised land.

The clock, carted from Prague, hazards an hour.
A neighbour's child appears, failed priest at eight
In shirt and table-runner; ruptures mass
From *Hänsel und Gretel*. Does his holy best
To trip her. Filches sugar, sausage. Spoils
Her apron-strings. She lets it all go by
With the same shrug she gave when the burst car
Refused to let us vamp it into life,
And her to church. Perhaps it was the same
In Hitler's thirties: the Sudeten farm
Left in a moment, and her history
Carried in paper bags beneath each arm.

Her face is like a man's: a Roman beak
Caesar might quail at; and the squat, square frame
An icon of compassion. As she turns
Towards the leaning light, behind her eye
Burn embers of Europe's foul allegory.
Her body bears its harsh stigmata, dug

With easy instruments of blood and bone.
And still, I'm certain, she could up and stick
A yelling pig, a priest, a partisan
With equal mercy. Or a lack of it.
She's wise as standing-stones. Her gift of years
Almost persuades belief in God, the Devil;
Their parallel unease. Both heaven and hell
Entirely unprepared for her arrival.

RICHARD BARTLETT

READING the ninety-year-old paper singed
By time, I meet my shadowed grandfather,
Richard Bartlett, stone-cutter, quarryman;
The Bible Christian local preacher, Sunday
School teacher and teetotaller. *Highly*
Respected, leading and intelligent
Member of the sect. He will be greatly missed.
Leaves wife and family of seven children,
The youngest being three months old.

Nine on a July morning: Richard Bartlett
About to split a stone, trying to find
A place to insert the wedge. The overhang
Shrugs off a quiet sting of slate. It nags
Three inches through the skull. Richard Bartlett
Never spoke after he was struck. Instead
Of words the blood and brains kept coming.
They lugged him in a cart to the Dispensary.
Never a chance of life, the doctors said.
He lived until twelve noon. His mate, Melhuish,
Searched for, but never found, the killing stone.
The fees of the jury were given to the widow.

The funeral was a thunder of hymns and prayers.
Two ministers, churchyard a checkerboard
Pieced with huge black: the family nudged nearer
The pit where the Workhouse was, and a leper's life
On the Parish. And in my grandmother
Was lit a sober dip of fear, unresting
Till her death in the year of the Revolution:
Her children safely fled like beads of mercury
Over the scattered map. I close the paper,
Its print of mild milk-chocolate. Bend to the poem,
Trying to find a place to insert the wedge.

DORA

MY LAST aunt, Dora Jane, her eye shrill blue,
The volted glance, the flesh scrubbed apple-clean,
Bullets for fingers, hair cut like a man,
Feet in a prophet's sandals, took the view
That work was worship; kept a kitchen share
In this her book of very common prayer.

She never called me Charles. Instead, the name
My father went by: Charlie. Who brought home
The war stowed in his body's luggage; died
In nineteen twenty-four. The strong wound bled
Unspoken in her heart, no signal tear
Disburdened on a waywardness of air.

One tale she prised from childhood. Prised again.
A brother and two sisters. How they ran
To the high field, through the tall harvest sea,
The stolen matches for a summer game.
As it was born, each pretty painted flame
Matching the sun's fire. And how suddenly

The youngest was a torch, and falling, falling,
Swathes of her long hair, and her burned voice calling.
Indifferent, the sun moved down the day:
The boy, my father, beating hand to bone
On the hard flame that struck a breath away
And turned a body and blood to a black stone.

Caught in her trap of years, Dora still told
Her tale, unvarying as granite. Held
Life at arm's length. And there were lovers, though
The clear blue gaze killed questioning. Revered
The tarot pack, fortunes in tea-cups. Feared
Nothing when it was time for her to go;

Half-smiled at me as sentimentalist.
The biscuit-tin clock thumping by her bed
Placed so that she could see the day drawl by.
Our only death, said Dora, is our first.
And she turned from me. But her winter eye
Spoke every word that I had left unread.

UNCLE STAN

HERE'S Uncle Stan, his hair a comber, slick
In his Sundays, buttoning a laugh;
Gazing, sweet-chestnut eyed, out of a thick
Ship's biscuit of a studio photograph.
He's Uncle Stan, the darling of our clan,
Throttled by celluloid: the slow-worm thin
Tie, the dandy's rose, Kirk Douglas chin
Hatched on the card in various shades of tan.

He died when I was in my pram; became
The hero of my child's mythology.
Youngest of seven, gave six of us his name
If not his looks, and gradually he
Was Ulysses, Jack Marvel, Amyas Leigh.
Before the Kaiser's war, crossed the grave sea
And to my mother wrote home forest tales
In Church School script of bears and waterfalls.

I heard, a hundred times, of how and when
The blacksmith came and nipped off every curl
('So that he don't look too much like a girl')
And how Stan tried to stick them on again.
As quavering children, how they dragged to feed
The thudding pig; balanced on the sty-beams,
Hurled bucket, peelings on its pitching head—
Fled, twice a day, from its enormous screams.

I watched the tears jerk on my mother's cheek
For his birth day; and gently she would speak
Of how time never told the way to quell
The brisk pain of their whistle-stop farewell:
A London train paused in the winter-bleak
Of Teignmouth. To his older friend said, 'Take
Good care of him.' Sensed, from a hedging eye,
All that was said when neither made reply.

I look at the last photograph. He stands
In wrinkled khaki, firm as Hercules,
Pillars of legs apart, and in his hands
A cane; defying the cold lens to ease
Forward an inch. Here's Uncle Stan, still game,
As Private, 1st Canadians, trimmed for war.
Died at Prince Rupert, B.C. And whose name
Lives on, in confident brass, for evermore.

That's all I know of Uncle Stan. Those who
Could tell the rest are flakes of ash, lie deep
As Cornish tin, or flatfish. 'Sweet as dew,'
They said. Yet—what else made them keep
His memory fresh as a young tree? Perhaps
The lure of eyes, quick with large love, is clue
To what I'll never know, and the bruised maps
Of other hearts will never lead me to.
He might have been a farmer; swallowed mud
At Vimy, Cambrai; smiling, have rehearsed
To us the silent history of his blood:
But a Canadian winter got him first.

THE BOOT MAN

'THIN AS sliced bacon,' she would say, fingering
The soles. 'They're for the Boot Man.' And I'd go
Up Crab Lane, the slight wafer of words she doled
Me out with worrying my tongue. *Please, soled*
And heeled by Saturday.

She didn't know
That given speech, to me, refused to come.
I couldn't read aloud in class; sat dumb
In front of howling print; could never bring
On my bitched breath the words I should have said,
Though they were pummelling inside my head.

Somehow the Boot Man stanched my speeches more
Than all the rest. He'd watch me as I tried
To retch up words: his eyes a wash-tub blue,
Stork-head held sideways; braces threaded through
Loops in his long-johns. Once again my dead
Father stood there: army boots bright as glass,
Offering me a hand as colourless
As phosgene.

And they told me time would cure
The irresolute tongue. But never said that I
Would meet again upon the faithless, sly
And every-morning page, the Boot Man's eye.

1940

JUNE 13TH, nine forty-five, the train
Seething. Tin adverts warming in the sun:
Monkey Brand Soap, Zebo, Sanatogen,
An empty chocolate-machine, its tongue
Stuck out. Beside the signal-box a blend
Of serious flowers. Torn posters: a North Coast
Too sweet with light, 22-carat sand,
Edged by unhungry seas. In second-best,
Glassed in the space between two lives, we test
The anxious air; file third-class cases on
The rack; observe the engine shake out pure
Blots of black water from its belly. Learn
Our travel-warrants off by heart. Wait for
The land to move; the page of war to turn.

ON LAUNCESTON CASTLE

WINDED, on this blue stack
Of downward-drifting stone,
The unwashed sky a low-
Slung blanket thick with rain,
I search the cold, unclear
Vernacular of clay,
Water and woods and rock:
The primer of my day.

Westward, a cardiograph
Of granite, Bodmin Moor;
Its sharp, uncertain stream
Knifing the valley floor.
Ring-dove and jackdaw rise
Over the blackboys' bell;
Circle, in jostling air,
The town's stopped carousel.

The quarry's old wound, plugged
With brambles is long-dry.
Dark bands of ivy scale
The torn school; lichens try
The building on for size.
Beyond the weir, a rout
Of barrack-tinted homes
Cancels a meadow out.

Down from the ribbed hill-crest
Combers of grasses ride.
Poppy, valerian
Bleed by the lean lake-side.
Allotments, in a slum
Of weeds and willows, keep
Scrupulous house. I note
A pinch of cows, of sheep.

Vociferous with paint,
A flock of ploughs supplies
Unlocal colour, where
The shut pond slowly dies.
Below the morning's saw-
Edged scope of birches, pines,
The hour is alchemised.
The hurt sun mends. It shines.

This was my summer stage:
Childhood and youth the play,
Its text a fable told
When time was far away.
But once I was too young
And still am too unsure
To cast a meaning from
The town's hard metaphor.

I cannot read between
The lines of leaf and stone,
For these are other eyes
And the swift light has gone.
By my birth-place the stream
Rubs a wet flank, breaks free
From the moored wall; escapes,
Unwavering, to sea.

AT THE CHURCH OF ST ANTHONY, LISBON

PLUMP AS a Christmas chicken, Fra Antonio
Throbs in the north aisle at a beach of candles;
Clutches, as hand luggage, a conker-coloured
Bible; three little sparking lilies. Handles
His uprising cooler than airline captains: dealing
One foot towards the faithful, a long gaze
Past the chipped saints and the once-painted ceiling
Up to the time-burnt dome, flayed pink and blue,
The burst glass, and the sharp light squinting through.

Tricked by an autumn change of clock, we come
To Mass an hour too soon. A sacristan
On saint-duty points, wordless, to the birth-
Place, marbled wall to wall, and scrubbed
Vanilla-white. It's like a hospital
For sin. Smells wickedly of wax. We scan
Pencilled memorials, prayers, winking stones.
The reliquary's heart of yellow bone
Bays like a brass-section. No sense of loss
That the saint's tongue is in another place.

Blessèd St Anthony, the silver speaker,
Patron of firemen, preacher to Muslims, fishes:
Who asked for, and received, nothing: for whom
The wild ass knelt before the Host as witness
To Christ within the Eucharist: eldest son
Of chaste St Francis, who woke in a vision,
The Child Jesus in his bright arms – the heart
Shies at the thought of your incarnate tongue,
Its taste of iron, of flowers, on my own;
My disbelief, its quiet comfort, gone.

In Padua the day you died, the children
Ran the white streets. Cried, 'Anthony is dead!
Our father Anthony!' And at your sainting
Bells rang, unbidden. On this Lisbon morning,
The Tagus furling into the quick bay,
A donkey, ballasted with guttering, passes.
Neither the time nor place for miracles!
It stops, but not to kneel, before the Host
Of huge stone over me. No magical
Message from Padua; the unpulled bells
Silently lurching high above my head.
St Anthony, our father, is not dead.

GUDOW

THE ROAD frays to a halt. A dyke
Of little frogs and Indian ink
Right-angles it. A ladder pinked
Half-wasting to a tree swings like
The hanged man. Restless, overhead,
A bird-hide drifts apart. A glass-
Faced cabin points to a distress
Of weeds and wildflowers, thickets mad

With recusant birds. Beyond a snarl
Of wire a parapet bleeds red sand
Where markers prick it. And beyond
Again, a top-shaped tower, a slick
Of nettle and thorn, shut bushes thick
With rattled wings, and grasses tall
As children. Through rain-needled air
The guards return our level stare.

Just visible, a small platoon
Of enemy cows moves forwards, back-
Wards through the mist's soft wall. A stick
Bursts underfoot. 'Morgen!' a road-man
Calls to the unseen wire patrol.
Grins, 'Never a reply.' The spring, meanwhile,
Advances, and the death-defy-
Ing cuckoo, heedless, beats the sky.

THE FIDDLER'S SON

WHEN I was a little lad
I lay within the cradle,
But through the living street I strolled
As soon as I was able.

There I met the King's young daughter,
She, too, walked the street.
'Come in, come in, little son of a fiddler.
Play me a tune sweet.'

It lasted scarcely a quarter of an hour.
The King he saw me singing.
'You rogue, you thief, what is that song
That to my child you're bringing?
In France there is a gallows built
Whereon you'll soon be swinging.'

In but the space of three short days
I had to climb the ladder.
'O give to me my fiddle to play,
For I'll not play hereafter.'

Then bowed I to, then bowed I fro,
On all the four strings telling.
A fine death lament played I,
And the King's tears were falling.

'My daughter is yours, little fiddler's son,
So to your bride come down.
In Austria is a castle built,
And you shall wear the crown.'

Anonymous: translated from the German

FRIEDRICH

FRIEDRICH, at twenty-two,
Sumptuously bankrupt,
Bought a garage:
Every fuel-tank ailing.

Also a mobilisation
Of motor-bikes. Owes
A butcher's ransom
Of Deutschmarks. Has bikes

In the bathroom, kitchen,
Closets, bedroom.
To use the landing lavatory you have
To aim between two Suzukis.

He's a graceful mover; slim as
A fern-tree. Has a dancer's
Small bottom. His wife Peachy's
A sorceress. They don't

Say much when I'm around
But I know they've something
Going between them better than
Collected Poems, a T.S.B. account,

Twelve lines in *Gems*
Of Modern Quotations
And two (not war) medals.
Today, Friedrich

Sat for three hours
Earthed by the ears
To a Sony Sound System.
I couldn't hear

The music, only
Him singing. It was like
A speared hog. *Love,*
Skirled Friedrich, *'s when a cloud*

Fades in the blue
'N there's me, 'n there's you.
'N it's true.
Peachy brings in Coke

And Black Forest *gâteau.*
Their mutual gaze
Broaches each other's eye.

Next week he'll be Vasco da Gama.

NEW YEAR'S EVE, ATHENS

OUTSIDE, Greek snow. I saw you in your room
Face-down, asleep. In black. An unstirred bed.
A figure measuring a marble tomb;
Like our respective loves, already dead.

The Greek Experience was packed and gone:
The sad, stilled caïque in Constitution Square
Rigged with toy lights, aground on paving-stone;
Dancing with cold beside its keel, a pair

Of stranded saints, each one a Nicholas
With boughs of red balloons, where yesterday
Tanks grumbled; resurrecting sentries pass-
Ing in and out of standing coffins grey

As brains or as bad thoughts; the women gift-
Wrapped for Epiphany: furs, patent-leather;
Poseidon's windy shrine in white sea-drift;
Byron's name scraped against the hurling weather;

High, unsweet goat-bells, and the shepherd's clear
Transistor clinking in the grove; the sure,
Strong silences of Delphi that declare
What should be, must be on the listening air.

Suddenly, thunder, and a midnight gun,
Stuttering rockets, shouts and songs. And then
Byzantine bells, jerking in unison,
Urged the year's breath. Whispered, 'Begin again.'

SLEEPER IN A VALLEY

COUCHED in a hollow, where a humming stream
Hooks, absently, sun-fragments, silver-white,
And from the proud hill-top beam falls on beam
Laving the valley in a foam of light,

A soldier sleeps, lips parted, bare his head,
His young neck pillowed where blue cresses drown;
He sprawls under a cloud, his truckle-bed
A spread of grass where the gold sky drips down.

His feet drift among reeds. He sleeps alone,
Smiling the pale smile that sick children wear.
Earth, nurse him fiercely! He is cold as stone,
And stilled his senses to the flowering air.

Hand on his breast, awash in the sun's tide
Calmly he sleeps; two red holes in his side.

translated from the French of Arthur Rimbaud

SONNET
AFTER JOACHIM DU BELLAY

for Alan Brownjohn

FLATTER a creditor with softest soap,
Charm the bank-manager, revive his hope,
Don't mention France and liberty, and when
You have to speak always first count to ten,

Don't botch your health with over-eating, -drinking,
Never let on exactly what you're thinking,
If you're in funds don't throw away the lot,
Guard a loose tongue when in some foreign spot,

Watch who would profit from you if they may,
Regard the mood and temper of each day,
Live with the world in harmony, hold fast
To sweetest freedom till you breathe your last:

All this has taken me, I blush to tell,
Three years to learn in Rome, my dear Morel.

DAN DORY

TODAY I saw Dan Dory
Walking out of the sea.
'Did you tell the world my story?'
Dan said to me.

Salt glittered on his breast, his fingers.
Drops of gold fell from his hair.
The look in his eye was sapphire-bright
As he stood there.

'Your head is white,' said Dan Dory.
'Trenched your face, your hand.
And why do you walk to greet me
So slowly across the sand?'

'I watched you held, Dan Dory,
In ocean fast.
Thirty, no, forty years ago
I saw you last.

'And now I see you older
By not a second's stroke
Than when the sun raged overhead
And the sea was flame, was smoke.'

'Did you tell the world my story?'
I heard him say.
'And for the unwisdom of the old
Do the young still pay?'

'Still spins the water and the land,'
I said, 'as yesterday'—
And leaned to take his hand. But he
Had vanished away.

NIGHT BEFORE A JOURNEY

BOOKS on the printed wall
Withhold their speech;
Pencil and paper and pen
Move out of reach.

The longcase clock in the hall
Winds carefully down.
No matter, says the house-ghost.
He is already gone.

A flower fallen on the shelf,
The stain of moon, of sun,
A wine-glass forgotten—
All await the return.

Nothing in the stopped house
Shall unbalance the air.
There is one, says the house-ghost,
Who is always here,

Patiently watching, waiting,
Moving from room to stilled room,
Light as breath, clear as light.
This, too, is his home.

When shall we meet, the stranger
And I, one with another?
When you leave for the last time,
Says the house-ghost. And together.

MAGPIE

'GOOD MORNING, Mr Magpie. How's your wife
Today?' I say. Spit on the risky air
Three times. The domino-coloured bird skips off
Through lodgepole pines, dry leaves of aspen poplar
Crisping the path.
                    You throw your head back, wear
For a splinter of time my hand in yours, and laugh
Aloud. And suddenly you say, 'You know
Aspen and poplar are the first to grow
After a fire?'
                    The Celt in me, unsafe
Before the magic bird, is hauling up
A rhyme from childhood. *One for sorrow, two*
For mirth. Three for a wedding . . . 'Magot pies'
Macbeth called them: they point out murderers,
Whose touch makes murdered blood flare out again.

The sun swims down the altered mountain; roughs
A gold line round your head. A wail of box-
Cars threads the valley as I try to scrape
My hand of blood, watching the magpie's track.
He struts in the dust. Bullies a whisky jack.

whisky jack: Canadian common grey jay

BANKHEAD

UNDER Cascade, its burn of ice,
We saw, as the swift day shut down,
Bitten in sandstone and black shale
The image of the vanished town.
Bankhead! The mine stopped like a tooth;
The unmade engine-house a mix
Of little stones and children's bricks;
Torn rail tracks, giant cacti; paths

From nowhere to nowhere; a scar
Of soil where a church stood, a school.
A burst lamp house. Then becomes now.
No sound but a thin creak of air.
The slow Albertan sky empties
Itself of light, slag-coloured. Trees
Shade into rocks and tipple. A steel
Bin offers its green gape to spill

The careful history of a town
Scraped like a polyp from the skin
Of Canada: of seven seams
Coiled in the land; a winter's tale
Subtle as methane, friable
As the coal, as love; of strikes, bad pay;
The homes at fifty dollars a room
Sold off, like hope, and sledged away.

Miners in tunics, caps, weighed down
With buffalo-horn moustaches gaze
Unsmiling from a photograph:
A vaguely military pose
With safety lamps. Two men stretch out
In foreground dirt like odalisques:
And every face an actor's mask
Hiding incertitudes of heart.

And still the valley dries the print
Of wounds upon its shroud of stone.
Impassive as Stoney or as Cree
The stiff rockface looks sheerly on.
Over the ridge there falls the grey
Cold voice of the coyote. As
I turn to touch your hand, your face,
I know such words as I might say
Must break like glass. And as we go,
Upon the vigilant mountain grow,
Unwatched, the first frail leaves of snow.

UNDER MOUNT RUNDLE

HERE COMES the little Cornishman, steering
West over the hard swamp and sedge, by winter
Birch and willow. 1841. He wears
Lamb's wool next the skin, a muster of shirts,
Lined trousers, leggings, pilot-coat, moccasins,
A sealskin cap screwed down against the weather.
He is the Reverend Robert Terrill Rundle
Aged 29: 'young, inexperienced,
Of no obvious fitness for his calling.'

His loves are missionising and the mountains.
Born, Mylor, parish of ilex, oak and water.
He flags a mile behind the sled; is disconcerted
At scrawls of blood on the snow from the beaten huskies;
At the delegation of Blackfoot—'so blackly painted
In history'—that greets him with kisses, prayers: the left
Hand given 'because it is nearest the heart'. The snow
Scores its harsh testament on the plain; goes missing.
He reads. Walks into the broken jaw of the Rockies.

HUSSAR

LEAVING Drumheller, a draft of desert air
Hustling the tumbleweed over the badlands;
Crossing the Red Deer River by the Atlas Mines,
Stone hoodoos stiff as mushroom-hatted janizaries
Slightly askew but braced for arms inspection,
The canyon in three flavours of red, green, gold,
We slithered the dirt road into corn country,
Grain silos in pastel colours, horizon of milk-cartons,
Small convoy of houses chancing the plain: R.C. church,
The Christmas lights at the ready in a smoulder
Of afternoon sun, four children thumping a ball,
Two dogs. At the settlement's rim, a sign blaring
Silently. *Hussar. Cultural Centre of Western Canada.*
The sky, the heavy light, pressing the pointed stake
Unremittingly into place; also the one gravestone,
A single tooth in the long yawn of the cemetery.

IN THE DOME CAR

THE TRAIN, as if departure were a state-
Secret, pulls out without a sound. I glance
Up from *The Globe and Mail* surprised to see
Through the dome car's dull window, Canada
Lurching quietly by. *Find the dome car,*
You said to me. *You'll see it all from there.*

And so I do. Or think I do. At first,
The Bow River, surface of china blue,
Indigo-coloured water squeezing through;
The rail-cars straightening in line ahead.
Giacometti trees like naked men
Stand, sky-high, in a littleness of snow;
Adverts for Honda, holidays (*Try us
Ski Jasper*); hunks of rock; the red Dutch barn
Recurring like a decimal; a thin
Smear of gold-leaf that is the coming corn.

In ice-edged light the train moves cautiously
Above a toy village, a clip of black
And white Indian ponies, a tepee
Hoisted beside a brake of pointed sticks.
A bridge hurries to meet us; spills across
A frozen lake. A car parked on the ice,
In shifting light, glitters a mile from shore.
We gape at it. But what I see is you
Walking the long nave of the train-station,
Never turning. *You'll see it all from there.*

We rush the stone horizon. At the last
Moment the mountains part; admit us to
Indian country, where the patient snow
Refuses the year's passage, scars the floor
Of a pale valley; lies in wait for more.

A TAMARACK GOOSE

OBSERVE this decoy goose made by
The Woodland Cree
Of scented bentwood broken
From the tamarack tree.

Two little shocks of larch
Make a hollow head
Clinched at the beak
With a tense delicacy of thread.

The body a delicious
Plumpness of twigs;
Neatly pollarded squab tail.
It stands on three legs.

A nothingness of mask and eye
Against the spring snows
Mimics the white cheek patch
Of the Canada goose.

When, at Epiphany,
I opened its gold box
There rose a fragrance
Of musk and sacred forest sticks.

I took the gift as a sign
Of trust, fidelity.
Hold on, have faith,
It seemed to say.

And so we did until the thin
Bond between us broke;
Neither having seen in the decoy goose
The joke.

AT THE CHÂTEAU LAKE LOUISE

THERE was no need of snow
To chill the valley's bone;
There was no need of ice
To wrap the naked stone.

Stilled by each other's blood
Silent, at last, we lay;
Watched as the winter sun
Rode down the day.

Nothing was said; no glance
Traded of ice or fire;
No shaft, it seemed, wounded
The usual air.

And each, with civil care
And words unspoken, thought
In separate silences
To unbruise the heart.

So we may never know,
Betrayer and betrayed,
In this small history
Which part was played.

Voiceless, the mountain smokes
Above the glacier wall,
Stubble of pine and fir,
The rigid waterfall.

Colours of lake and sky
Pale in lost light;
Ebb to simplicities
Of black, of white.

UNTITLED

THAT slender boy of fifteen
in a soft *sfumato* of crayon,
cap dragged down to his eyebrows,
eyes moist and still—his irises dark
and shy; those cheeks dusty as the skin
of apricots; this long-haired Euryalus
perfumed with lemon, needs his Nisus,
but fate has assigned him to a different
day, where, mildly confused, timid and
drowsy, he now poses before Raphael,
to become an ephemeral drawing,
a self-indulgent *ritratto di sé medesimo*
quando giovane, even though the painter
was all of 27 years.

translated from the Serbo-Croatian of Hamdija Demirović

LEGEND

SNOW-BLIND the meadow; chiming ice
Struck at the wasted water's rim.
An infant in a stable lay.
A child watched for a sight of Him.

'I would have brought spring flowers,' she said.
'But where I wandered none did grow.'
Young Gabriel smiled, opened his hand,
And blossoms pierced the sudden snow.

She plucked the gold, the red, the green,
And with a garland entered in.
'What is your name?' Young Gabriel said.
The maid she answered, 'Magdalene.'

ROCCO

I AM St Roche's dog. We stand
Together on the painted wall:
His hat tricked with a cockleshell,
Wallet and staff in pilgrim hand.
He lifts a torn robe to display
The plague-spot. I sit up and wait.
A lot of us has peeled away.
My breed is indeterminate.
Bow ! Wow !

Under a Piacenza sun
The sickness struck him like a flame.
'Dear Lord,' he cried, 'my life is done!'
And to a summer forest came.
But I, his creature, sought him high
And sought him low on his green bed
Where he had lain him down to die.
I licked his wounds and brought him bread.
Bow ! Wow !

And he was healed, and to his house
Sick by the hundred seethed and swarmed
As, by God's grace, the Saint performed
Cures that were quite miraculous.
Now my good master's home is where
Are heavenly joys, which some declare
No fish nor bird nor beast may share.
Ask: Do I find this hard to bear?
Bow ! Wow !

RETURNING SOUTH

FIVE DAYS since I left Cornwall. Sunday bells.
The moor scraped with a February dole
Of sun. Road-signs to Glastonbury, to Wells
Vague with snow-fume. The cold hunch of Brent Knoll
Heavily salted. Fields white as the pole
Through Wiltshire. Then on the windscreen a slow
Small-change of copper-coloured mud. Heathrow.

A Qantas strike. We're ten lost tribes, and tote
Our luggage round the clanging hall as though
Panzer divisions were at the gate.
I dump bags at the check-in. Scratch a note
Already written to no matter who.
Swallow a Scotch. Am launched too late, too soon
At forty-five degrees against the moon.

Bahrain. The sun-god floats above the town.
Eden of poets, pearls! I squinny at
Sumerian verse on plastic tablets. Two
Young sheikhs in lily robes come willowing down
The stairs. Next flight, Damascus. A prayer-mat
Wags from the airport mosque. I wander through,
Touching a silence radical as dew.

At Singapore a steam-iron heat: a scald
Cooling to Melbourne, where we rise, undead,
Above unintimate squares of green and red.
City in hock: near-prisoner of the bald
Shine that's Port Phillip Bay. Unjacketed,
I chuck cash, keys on the still-falling shelf.
Unpack shirts, socks. *Dear Christ, what's this? Myself.*

BEECHWORTH

STEPPING OUT of the sun's clear tide,
Shaking off drops of light, of heat,
The cellar's dark-blue box of air
Envelops me, tempers my cheek:
A drift of air thinned from the Pole,
Although the month is March, and the
Australian autumn newly born,
Thumped on the bottom, given safe
Conduct to swift, reluctant life.

Behind the grille, a dusty show
Of handcuffs, helmets, an off-white
Anthology of emu bones,
Tin boxes, lamps, a Cobb & Co.
Coach ticket: Melbourne–Bendigo.
The thick bole of an Albion press
Turns, slow as iron, into Zeus
Aiming a finger at the small
Set-piece: a granite prison-cell.

Through a locked door of chicken-wire
A sick bulb challenges the sun
A step away, and corpse-cold air.
And there—My God! But how the heart
Suddenly jars!—a figure lies
In primrose light on an old bed:
A boy, asleep, under a loam-
Grey blanket; the sham, black-haired head
Sharp-angled from the body's frame.

A presage innocent, unspoken,
Of the death-mask, and how the rope
Squirmed tight-shut underneath an ear:
'The bulge shows where the neck was broken';
A rusty bucket, poised between
A chair, a child's white, chipped commode;
A twist of stairs that leads up to
The court-house. A card makes it plain:
'Kelly first gaoled here, aged sixteen'.

Outside, I quietly resume
The sun, among a tarnish of
Rakes, harrows, boilers long unboiled,
Stilled engines—the heart's engine still
Hurrying. Don't want to wake him's my
Excuse, or wake within myself
The necessary response, or hear
The head's dark question, and the sly
Evasions of the heart's reply.

Days drop like leaves; silt the fine shaft
Of years from here to Melbourne Gaol.
I pick a smash of mirror up.
It shows me who I'm not; hides what's
To be, as Ned's epiphany
Burns pure as wax. He rises. Sings.
Stands, noosed and white-capped, on the drop.
Adjusts the rope's scarf. Declares, *Such
Is life.* But knows that it is not.

PINCHGUT

SOON after Hiroshima
Three dozen years ago
(As might be three dozen thousand)
Upping and downing past the Heads
Into Sydney Harbour
Eyes on the bridge's grey protractor
Laid against the city and the sky,
I missed a sight of Pinchgut
The broad-arrow island where convicts
Putrefied or, attempting to escape,
Were shark-snapped or strangled
By ropes of water.

This morning, my back to the giant
Hand of oyster-shells
Jammed in a cement beach
(Today, *Madame Butterfly*)
I glimpse the punishing lump
As I take the ferry
To Manly Fun Pier:
Famed for Fun since '31,
Seven miles from Sydney
And a thousand miles from care.

Three trainee-nuns in white and blue
Congeal on a life-raft
Out of the sun's blast
Under a health warning:
Kiss a non-smoker
And enjoy the difference.

I am seeking a sign.
Any kind of sign.
I lurch the deck,
Legs throbbing in concert with the Diesels.
A wartime unease
At skimming over the slum roofs of the sea
Threatens a return.

On the bulkhead a moving hand has written,
Jesus jogs.

THE DANCERS

TO A clearing
in the foyer
at the Gallery
of Art,
and a chatter
of spectators
waiting for the show
to start,
five young men, black,
naked, dotted
white and daddy-long-
legs thin
out of forty
thousand years of
dreamtime came lightfoot-
ing in.
Ssss! hissed the dancers from Arnhem Land.

And a primal
stillness fell as
when arose the earl-
iest sun,
each dancer an
emblem painted
on rockface, or scored
in stone.
With an unpre-
meditated
seemliness they took
the floor,
staring sightless
as is lightning
through a bronze by Hen-
ry Moore.
Ssss! hissed the dancers from Arnhem Land.

To an insect
buzz of music,
snap of sticks, high nas-
al whine,
touched with brown and
saffron ochre,
and their teeth a yell-
ow shine,
five young men came
barefoot, dancing—
the sun halting in
its climb—
effortlessly,
forwards, backwards
through the littoral
of time.
Ssss! hissed the dancers from Arnhem Land.

Beaded and in
feather bracelets
to the hoarse-voiced didge-
ridoo,
they were emu
and echidna,
swirling snake and kang-
aroo;
razoring this and
that way sharply,
swifter than the bush-
fire flame,
each a demon,
each an angel,
each a god without
a name.
Ssss! hissed the dancers from Arnhem Land.

Suddenly the
dance was ended,
clocks took back the Mel-
bourne day,
and it was as
if the dancers
melted like a mist
away.
In the restaur-
ant I saw them,
serious, and at smil-
ing ease:
five young men in
T-shirts, jeans, with
pavlovas and five
white teas.
Ssss! hissed the dancers from Arnhem Land.

IN A MELBOURNE SUBURB

'THE LAST hot day,' the Italian fruiterer said,
Proving his own bad grapes. Carlton in March.
A Wedgwood sky. Façades of houses whorled,
Fluted like plaster wedding-cakes, and scabbed
Pure black. Bristles of grass. A hand-out, whirled
By traffic says, 'Save Carlton,' but from what
Is not vouchsafed. Cacti, caged and half-caged
On balconies surrender bits of flesh
To sidewalks. Cartons, tickets, Coke tins scurf
The road's hard scalp. What passes as a bed
Of white flowers on waste-sprinkled ground takes off,
Lands, and re-forms: squadron of silver gulls.
In autumn gardens khaki campbells pray
From plastic pools for rain. Two Yugoslavs
Sweat out Saturday's footy, as the sound
Of children singing 'Mrs Murphy's Chowder'
Seeps from a junior school. I seat myself
Beneath this vast, anonymous, southern tree.
Think: now's the time to catch a poem; search
For bait; remain relaxed; prepare to cast
A blue line on the afternoon's clear page.

The last hot day. Too soon the swivelling breeze
Assumes another course; from north, from south.
The warm springs of the heart begin to freeze;
The lip and tongue quietly dry with drouth.
High overhead renaissance clouds drift by
In line along an overspread of sky.
I reel the bare catch in. It is the same.
A voice from half a world away. A name.

GREEK ORTHODOX, MELBOURNE

THE CHURCH leaks yellow light; a scent
Of drooling wax. A priest hurls in,
Suddenly pitches his black tent,
Scolds God in Greek. The skewer-thin
Acolyte in red trainers tugs
His lace aside, chews gum, prepares
White smoke. Christ from his icon stares
Blackly at ribbons, painted eggs
Smudging in children's hands. Outside,
Circus-high on a rainy tower,
The priest appears bearing the fire,
And Christ is risen. Bells collide
Not quite together. Handshakes, smiles,
Embraces as the last tram fails
To make the depôt, braked by strong
Prayer and thunderflash; a ring
Of dancers. Rockets rip the dark
Sky's cloth. The stems of candles spark
Into gold flowers: each careful flame
Shielded and carried wavering home
For the year's blessing and Christ come.
The church, bricked-out in patterns of
The cross, glows like a lantern. I
Watch the white walls, the rising sky,
How every coloured window prints
Brash histories of death and love.
Nothing is there of certainty.
Ah, how the wicked mosaic glints
In St Nektarios's eye!

KITE, POISONED BY DINGO BAIT

Trephina Gorge, Northern Territory

BY THEN the creek had died, and splashed
Sand, fine as pepper, at our feet.
Ghost gums, their leaves nervously green,
Glistened like mercury in the heat.
The gorge opened its wound of rock,
Immaculate in the day's long glare.
Gobbets of stone lay where they fell
In dreamtime through original air.
Liquorice-coloured flies blundered
Expertly, always out of reach.
Wild passion-fruit, half-eaten by
Cockies and ants rubbished the beach.
Spinifex pigeons waddled, swam
From a small shore as bright as bone;
And unsweet in the waterhole:
A cow, its ribs a xylophone.
Wild donkeys, elegantly buffed,
Arrowed a glance and danced away;
Rumped on a naked river gum,
A kite, as motionless as clay.
Plumping its feathers against death
Like northern birds against the frost
It gripped the noon, its eye of stone
Blinded as by a pentecost.

Abandoning the sour pool, we
Slopped through lagoons of desert grit
Back to the truck—ex-Vietnam,
Still camouflaged—hoping to hit
The beef road to Arltunga. Red
Bulldust made smoke behind us, and
Thinned for a moment, to reveal,
Etched on a plate of scrub and sand,
The cow, heaving comfortably
Into the waterhole. The spry
Donkeys skittering back. The kite
Gleaned from the bough, and shadow-sly
Another in the unversed sky.

GLEN HELEN

SHAVING BY torchlight and the webbed window,
Moths butting my lip, my cheek, morning unrisen,
I watch the invisible sky: a graph of dingoes,
Birdsquawk, and donkeys loud as New Year sirens.
The sun inserts a single blade of light
Into the bag of dark; advances low
Over the scrub and sand. Strikes the gorge-side.
It glows in fifty shades of red. The day ignites.

Cardboard cut-outs along the waterhole
Slowly reveal themselves as pelicans.
Divider-stiff, wading birds stab the map
Of corrugated water. The day's finger
Sharpens the skeletons of the ranges: crouched
Frilled lizards, frozen dinosaurs. We pick
Our way among burst cans and cushions,
The carapaces of old cars: pellets
Spat out by delicate monsters. Make a joke
About sand-tyres; finding the bitumen.

And underneath our jaunting tongues is this:
How both of us came, hand in cooling hand,
To the stone centre of the wilderness.
Drank from a single cup. Shared fortune; bed.
Pretended not to notice how love bled
Into the eager sand. Lay, heart on heart:
Yet never slept so cold, so far apart.

ALICE SPRINGS

A HIGH May sky, pale blue and faintly brushed
With strokes of cloud. The river-line a gash
Of beer-cans, gums; a froth of broken glass.
A fun-fair grinds the empty afternoon
To months of Sundays, and the fat drunk dances
Silently by the children's carousel.
Anglo-Saxons in shorts and thongs prospect
The flea-market. A black boy (his front teeth
Removed, therefore initiated) politely
Enquires the time: but time is out of hand,
Lost to bright forces subtler than sand.

Sturt's desert rose: *Gossypium sturtii*,
Bakes by the peeling obelisk (part black
Part white), *Lest We Forget*, on Anzac Hill.
In the half-fallen sun a doze of camels
Wilting with awful patience. A detritus
Of boomerangs and bells and whips and saddles.
Blow-ups of Afghan drivers, angry-whiskered;
Tribesmen on stilted bones. Landscape: an aching
Pepper of copper-coloured boulders; all
Grown small before the backdrop of the ranges,
The air surly with dust as the light changes.

And in the Pitchi-Ritchi gardens, tablets
To local deities: *Camp Oven Doll,*
Famous for hospitality. Could run up
A Christmas dinner out of mulga bark
And spinifex. Their chariots: '*Pearl of the West*',
Of Western Queensland and the Birdsville track.
Named bullockies who with their teams and wagons
Braved floods and sandstorms and the heat of summer
To keep the town of Stuart (re-named Alice)
With goods from the rail-end at Oodnadatta.
Their names are light; letter by winking letter,
Easing mythologies out of the wild stone,
New dreamtime from a stubbornness of water.

ROSS RIVER

STANDING at the cabin door,
Morning unlatching the day,
I watch for the timorous
Four-foot lizard's arrival
For a bit of tucker.
The matchbox radio fries up
News from Europe: Death of Tito,
Iranian Embassy Siege Lifted.

Down by the creek, galahs
In primary colours part the simple air
Over the green and yellow Egyptian reeds,
The red wet sand,
Next to a dolour of car bodies,
Gas and beer cans, dead tyres.
Under an awning, Aphrodite,
Beautiful in washed-out
Khaki shirt and pants
Strips a camp bed, airs the linen,
Is frying bacon: the fat
Explosive as static.

Her young Texan, bush-hatted,
John the Baptist whiskered,
Leads in two camels
He has netted in the Simpson Desert;
Sees the pen in my hand.
'Score, America three,'
He says. 'What's yours,
Poet?'

ECHUNGA

To Jeanne and Brian Matthews

UNDER A cloister of stringy-barks, rosellas
Dipping in line ahead, an illustration
From a frail map's border, *terra australis*
Incognita, dust jumping where the pick-up
Swats the scraped road, I watch as from an ocean
Of sallow grass the homestead surfaces
Among the masts of eucalypt. Echunga.
A place near by. Somewhere, buried from sight,
The Murray: 'Come a thousand miles and looks it,'
You say, serving the bread, the white cold wine.

Caught in the early sights of the acacia
I walk the spread. What seems a West Penwith
Light glitters, and the kookaburra seizes
A length of still, blue air; shakes it. Grasshoppers
Flip gracelessly, like brown wood-chips. The sun
Fries down, and skink and stumpytail fluster
From underfoot. Birds on wire twigs abrade
Smooth silences with their complaints. The dam
Opens an oily eye, and at its rim:
Reeds thick enough to hide a Moses in.

A shattered gum lugubriously points
Four ways south, where the sea bites: to a throw
Of homes between us and the pulled-down sky.
Slow rocks turn into drifts of sheep; cattle
Become uneasy stones. Over the hills'
Green barbican, a gulf of carbon where
The bushfire came the day that you expected
The flame to vault the scar; the trees exploding
Ahead of its fast tide. Shadows were blue,
The children told me. Smoke coloured the sun.

And then, you say, just as you all were loading
Paintings, kids' fishing-rods into the car,
Wind and flame suddenly turned, leaving a taste
Of smoke; wry tears wrenched on the cheek.

Today
I see the naked-footed children trawl
The dam for yabbies, and I watch you clinging
Together, minute-long, before I'm driven
Back to the airport. And it is as though
You fear—one, both of you—another kind
Of fire within this Eden, or blood broken
Under the hard sun. The incurious blue, still burning
Over the homestead roof. The sprinkler turning.

MANJIMUP

WE COME, the two of us, to Manjimup,
Walking the endless naves of jarrah and redgum,
Shoes smudged with wet loam the colour of blood.
At One Tree Bridge a single kookaburra

Machine-guns the noon light. The cormorant
Casts over the rigid pool its barb of eyes.
Somewhere beyond the rocks and rushes, a bright
Secrecy of maidenhair fern, the stream fidgets

Through sharp stones. We emerge into the kingdom
Of the blue wren, the golden whistler, bees
In a sudden bank of rosemary, curt grasses
Silver-grey, laden with water. The rainbow

Perfect as a child's picture, launches itself
Across a slate sky. 'A nice stand of young karri,'
You say, pointing beyond the jarrah flowing down
The valley towards the hills where the karri begins:

Half-hidden by drifts of blue rain. Ahead,
The blue rain as we move, the two of us, from where
The dryness of jarrah comes to a sudden stop:
You, in another season; I in Manjimup.

COTTESLOE BEACH

FROM India the swimming sea
Touches the shelf of sand,
Gathers a salt, tremendous breath,
Takes a run at the land.
Unceasing on the constant shore
I hear the waters fray,
With rushing speech of stone and shell
Fall back on the bay.

A sky like blacking scrubs the light
Of all but a thin star.
The wind tosses the sheeted sand
Over wire-grass and scar.
I walk the tideline, its rough mark
Of salt and bitter weed.
Shameless, the beach opens its page
For all to read.

At my right hand the sea erupts;
At my left, the tall
Window, bright with ticking flame,
Pictures on the wall.
Someone runs to the mailbox.
A taxi whines by.
Two lovers stand illumined
In its slow eye.

Soon, soon the ocean
Cools the heart's blood to snow;
Blurs with its breath the globe of air
As I turn to go.
Within the sea's dark voice I hear
Another's, long unvisited.
Sleepless, I listen for the light,
The star still glittering in my head.

IN THE PINNACLES DESERT

SOUTH OF Cervantes, Thirsty Point, wedges
Of capstone galling the track, drumming the gut
Of the four-wheel drive, we cross a sabre-cut
In the scrub. *The Namban River*, I read.
Flows only in winter, ending in a swamp
Near the coast. I raise my eyes. Beyond ridges
Of sand, fine Chinese white, a mess of shell-
Grit, frosted with salt, the sea unrolling
Bolts of long water, and its great bell tolling

Across the Pinnacles, goliath-high,
Facing every which way. Overhead
A cloud flaps free; spatters pink sand with red.
Here, where the ice-cap melted and returned
Its tithe of water to the sea, the mad
Rocks lean against the wind. They calcify
As ogham stones inscribed by storm and sun;
Bones of the archaeopteryx; the towers
Of mad kings; stairways delicately spun.

Are Easter Island profiles; swollen pin-
Cushions; the improbable arm or hand
Of buried heroes bursting through the sand.
A kangaroo sprints from its scrape of clay.
The emu hunts for seeds. The anchored cray-
Boats swing like metronomes. I see the print
Of the wild-turkey's claw in the dry spine
Of the river-bed first named for Frederick Smith,
Died near this place in 1839

After shipwreck. *Later, re-named Namban.*
The spice-sailors, cruising beyond the reef
Saw a ruined city, and this glittering sheaf
Of stones its monuments. A darkening sun
Slants on the palm, the blackboy tall as a man
Unloosing its gross head of sharpened hair.
Small leaves of rain drift from the sky's tall tree
On the grounded seaman, the failed river named
For Frederick Smith, that will not reach the sea.

AT KENNET RIVER

DRIVING through Separation Creek
I stopped at Kennet River, where
The Tasman in a fury slammed
Breakers house-high upon the sand.

Between the fire-break and the bay
The house took cover from the trees;
The white scent of the eucalypt
Insinuating the salt breeze.

Easter. In the upside-down sky
Fresh wounds of light, and from a far
Ambush of stone a single bird
Scarred with sharp cries the ebony air.

And as I slept and as I woke
A voice within another strove.
'Thus far . . . thus far. . . .' it seemed to say
In tones discreet and soft as love.

It was the civil-speaking sea
Whispering in its cage of glass,
As night to its new-risen mast
Nailed a rough crucifix of stars.

Early, through Separation Creek,
I went the way that I had come:
The envious flood squirming beside
Me, biding its green tide; its time.

A SONG OF TRUTH

WHEN Christ the Lord of Heaven was born
Cold was the land.
His mother saw along the road
A fig-tree stand.
'Good Mary, leave the figs to grow
For we have thirty miles to go.
The hour is late.'

Mary came near unto the town.
Stayed at a door.
Said to the little farmer, 'Pray
Let us stay here.
Not for myself these words I make
But for an infant child's sake.
The night is chill.'

The farmer opened up his barn.
Bade them go in.
When half the winter night had gone
Came there again.
'Where you are from in this wide world,
And are not killed by winter cold,
I cannot tell.'

The farmer came into his house
The barn beside.
'Rise up, dear wife,' he cried, 'and may
Best fire be made
That these poor travellers are warm
And safe from wind and weather's harm
Here at our hearth.'

Smiling, Mary then entered in
The farmhouse door;
Also her good and gentle man
That self-same hour
Drew from his pack a crock of tin.
With snow the young child filled it fine,
And it was flour.

Crystals of ice he placed therein
As sugar rare
And water that white milk should be
Both fresh and fair.
Over the flame they hung the crock,
And such soft sweetness did they cook,
Was finest pap.

Of wooden chip the good man carved
With homely blade
A spoon that was of ivory
And diamond made.
And now the child does Mary sweet
Give of the pap that He may eat:
Jesus His name.

translated from the German: 'A Song of Truth' (*Ein Wahrheitslied*) was published for the first time in *Des Knaben Wunderhorn* (1806–8), in which a number of the ballads were written by the editors themselves, Clemens Brentano and Achim von Arnim.

BAMBOO DANCE

THEY dance, the Filipino boy,
    The Filipino girl, between
The clapping bamboo that would break
    An innocence of blood and bone.

In the hot light, to drum and flute,
    Clear of the bamboo trap they leap.
It is as if they swim in air.
    Music, like water, bears them up.

Barefoot, barelegged, flesh opaline
    As is the secret shell, they move
Their easy bodies to inscribe
    The dusk with characters of love.

And still the bamboo-holders bring
    The poles together like a shot;
Swifter the ever-restless drum,
    The sharp insistence of the flute.

The dance is love, love is the dance
    Though bamboo shocks their dancing day.
Ceases. Smiling, the dancers go,
    Hand locked in gentle hand, their way.

FABLE

I WAS A slave on Samos, a small man
Carelessly put together; face a mask
So frightful that at first the people ran
Away from me, especially at dusk.

I was possessed, too, of a rattling tongue
That only now and then would let words pass
As they should properly be said or sung.
In general, you could say I was a mess.

One thing redeemed me. People marvelled at
The brilliance with which my speech was woven.
It was, they said, as if a toad had spat
Diamonds. And my ugliness was forgiven.

Soon I was freed, and sooner was the friend
Of kings and commoners who came a-calling.
Of my bright hoard of wit there seemed no end,
Nor of the tales that I rejoiced in telling.

But there were heads and hearts where, green and cold,
The seeds of envy and of hate were lying.
From our most sacred shrine, a cup of gold
Was hidden in my store, myself unknowing.

'Sacrilege! He is thief!' my accusers swore,
And to the cliffs of Delphi I was taken,
Hurled to the myrtle-scented valley floor
And on its whitest stones my body broken.

'This is the end of him and his poor fame!'
I heard them cry upon the gleaming air.
Stranger, now tell me if you know my name,
My story of the Tortoise and the Hare?

BUGIS STREET

OVER OUR heads long skeins of light
Fly Bugis Street, each lamp a white
Bulging eyeball. We sit out on
The buckled strip of hosed-down stone
Silted with chairs and tables; stare
Like children at a country fair
That smells of sea-damp, joss-sticks, drains.

Music discharges like a gun.
I drink a Tiger beer. You take
A coffee laced with ginger; make
No comment as the girls parade
In polished gowns, spangles, gilt shoes,
Ear-rings as long as icicles
And scalloped wigs in dangerous shades

Of lollipop. On each slant face
The necessary mask of pure
Defiance; a sharp mouth that trades
The ritual obscenities
With those who pass unseeing; dare
To mock the solemn ordinance,
The painted glance that fails to hide,

Somehow, a terrible innocence.
Pedlars flicker among the crowd
With cassettes, T-shirts, watches, loud
Pictures in silk of matadors;
And for a dollar Singapore
Photographs of the girls. But they
Are boys. The stars are glass. The sea

A cauldron of voices. The moon's ray
A searchlight crawling on the bay.
We leave. A pedlar blocks our path;
Reads every word I do not say,
Pushes an orchid dunked in gold
Across the dirty tablecloth
And my hand shakes, but not with cold.

IN MALACCA

I SAW St Francis Xavier today
As I went through the Santiago Gate:
Stone-faced, stone-frocked, fisherman's arms apart
As if to show the one that got away
To the slow farmer with the bullock cart,
The sailboat crossing, re-crossing the strait,
The dredger swallowing the level bay.

On ticket of leave from the Arts Festival
(Doing Malaysia in half a day)
I plant the page with words; attempt a print
Of gilt-voiced temples, a brown waterfall,
The elephant-headed god in Goldsmith Street
—Four-handed, mover of obstacles—intent
On smiling sleep, a rat across his feet.

Safe in their trope of forest leaves a pair
Of spider-monkeys sip the critical air
Where softly in the paper jungle wait
The patient tiger and the five-step snake.

FLYING

FLYING over the crumpled hide of Spain,
Seville to Barcelona, the pinned-out skin
Curing in dusty light, I watch a thin
Skein after endless skein of road, mule-track
Thread the wild secrecy of valleys, lap
Impossible hills, and on the sudden plain
Meet other paths; as swiftly part again.

The Moorish castle spoils above the town.
Houses, spilt sugar-lumps, coagulate
Around a church half-eaten by sun. A neat
Gethsemane of olives, grey as slate,
Spreads like a shadow. Stubs of rock stitch lean
Watercourses, sand-beds, in slanting heat.
The land aches with the first green thrust of wheat.

So much to blunt the eye! And still I hear
The squealing bands behind the *pasos*: stare
At porters shouldering wounded Jesus down
Holy Week; the unblemished penitents,
Masked, in fools' caps; the Holy Virgin fenced
By thickets of candle-flame, her shaken crown
A foliage of stars, her wax tears spent.

The ladder-man adjusts the soldier's lance,
Re-lights dead candles, fixes Pilate's cloak.
Crowds flood the Avenida like a dam.
I squat by the cathedral on a rung
Of broken stone. And suddenly the young
Gypsy from the Trianas, peddling coke,
Smiles frankly, makes to pass me by, but first
Runs through me with brilliant, uncasual glance.
Sees me for what I was, for what I am.
Offers a cup. Having observed my thirst.

MY NAME IS MARTIN OXBOY

MY NAME is Martin Oxboy,
Ploughman,
Of this earth and woody parish.
I am a young man of quite exceptional ugliness:
The hairs of my head the colour and feel of burnt meat.
My eyes planted a hand's-breadth apart.
My nose flat as a stretch of sand just ironed by the tide.
My sniffers wide as a pair of sea-caves near the same.
My lips are two strips of undercooked beef.
My teeth, a boneyard of neglected yellow tombstones.
Observe, too, my fashionable dress.
(He whirls about and displays it: bull's-hide
boots, gaiters bound to above the knee with rope,
and a reversible cloak—one side even rougher
than the other.)
And this, my accoutrement.
(Raises his great club over his head.)
What an equipage for a boy-chap
In search of a good place in society!
Not to mention a suitable mate.
God be blessed that I'm sprung from a good family.
My great-great-grandaddy lived in Genesis Street;
Went travelling after he'd a-accidentally
Killed his younger brother as was a cow-keeper
And very religious. Settin' fire to a sacrifice
He was, at the time.
My old Auntie Jezzie, bit of a princess,
Painted her face up like a picture
On a church wall
Down at the east end.
Fell out of a window, she did, poor old soul—
Must have been givin' the sill a wipe over.
And there's my Uncle Jone:
Signed on in the barque *Gospel Marine*
As a sea-lawyer;
Jumped overboard in a typhoon

To lighten the load
And took a second passage in the guts of a crocodile
Or some such fish.
Well, now, what's to be expected of me—
With such ancestry?
Think yourselves lucky, mates.
You come purling off quite another
Set of palm trees.
Character, that's what it takes
To overcome my lot.
But I got plenty o' that.
Dainty as a daisy, I am, underneath this rummage
Of wool and skin.
  (He looks about the forest.)
My God, but nature's wonderful!
You got to work among it to know it.
See that pretty butterfly?
No it ain't. It's a moth;
Gettin' a mite dimmit, it is.
A moth. An' tremblin'.
Delicate as a baby's tongue.
Look at them tame and tender colours!
Landed on a leaf, it has.
(Appreciatively) Ah!
  (He gazes at it, drooling.
  Suddenly brings his club up and over his head and deals it a smashing blow.)
(Sadly) Poor little animal. Looked sickly, it did.
(Instantly cheerful.) Eased it out of this world of sadness and sufferin', that's what. It's happy now.

from the verse-play 'The Ballad of Aucassin and Nicolette'

BOULGE

EDWARD FITZGERALD sleeps
Under this sheet of stone,
Neat as never in life,
Innocent, alone.

The earth that he lies in is his.
Grass and willow-herb drown
The wilderness path through the trees.
The great house is down.

He longed to lie in birdsound.
To be ash. To dare
The salt of the ocean and find
Lodging there.

Flint-eyed, the church, the tower
Shadow his page.
Thinly the Persian rose
Frets in its cage.

It is He that hath made us. And he
Who is lying among
Hard voices of pebble and shard
Holds his tongue.

DICK LANDER

WHEN WE were children at the National School
We passed each day, clipped to the corner of
Old Sion Street, Dick Lander, six foot four,
Playing a game of trains with match-boxes.

He poked them with a silver-headed cane
In the seven kinds of daily weather God
Granted the Cornish. Wore a rusted suit.
It dangled off him like he was a tree.

My friend Sid Bull, six months my senior, and
A world authority on medicine,
Explained to me just what was wrong with Dick.
'Shell-shopped,' he said. 'You catch it in the war.'

We never went too close to Dick in case
It spread like measles. 'Shell-shopped, ain't you, Dick?'
The brass-voiced Sid would bawl. Dick never spoke.
Carried on shunting as if we weren't there.

My Auntie said before he went away
Dick was a master cricketer. Could run
As fast as light. Was the town joker. Had
Every girl after him. Was spoiled quite out

Of recognition, and at twenty-one
Looked set to take the family business on
(Builders' merchants, seed, wool, manure and corn).
'He's never done a day's work since they sent

'Him home after the Somme,' my Uncle grinned.
'If he's mazed as a brush, my name's Lord George.
Why worry if the money's coming in?'
At firework time we throw a few at Dick.

Shout, 'Here comes Kaiser Bill!' Dick stares us through
As if we're glass. We yell, 'What did you do
In the Great War?' And skid into the dark.
'Choo, choo,' says Dick. 'Choo, choo, choo, choo, choo,
choo.'

SUNDAY SCHOOL OUTING

They always say
He's fond of little children.
Liza Tremlett, lives next the church,
Punishing her front door-step
With a bass broom
Casts a laser eye
Into the God-filled sky.
A sky like coal.

It is the once-a-year day
Of the Outing
To sand and sea.
Breathless, we scale
Sam Prout's aboriginal
'Queen of Cornubia'
Parked between St Cyprian's
And the conker tree.

The vicar, camouflaged
In sea-side suit
And straw boater
Going yellow
Reads out the roll
Checking for stowaways.
Boys in braces, knee-length
Stockings and sandals.

Girls with ribbons,
Cotton-frocks like bell-tents
With flowers on.
Pasties, Thermoses, spades,
Tin buckets, cuts of lemon
For fallible travellers.
Lightning razors
The heavy air.

They always say
He's fond of little children,
Says Liza, voice of granite.
Well, now's His chance.
The 'Queen of Cornubia'
Lurches uneasily into the eager,
Quite unrelenting
All-day rain.

THIS CLOCK

THIS CLOCK belonged to Maisie. I first heard
Its shrill tick, like the beat of a too-swift
Mineral heart the night my mother and I
Went to the Big House for the washing. We
Sat by the kitchen range while Maisie packed
The flasket tight as a boulder, the tin clock
Pelting split seconds from the mantelshelf.

The only servant in that ugly house
With its own blackvoiced rookery, Maisie was
My mother's Friend: wire-thin, her face as pale
As a submariner's, hands rubbed so clean
The light shone through them, hard apron and cap,
Stockings field-grey and flat black shoes with straps.

Sharp-faced, voice barely a whisper, Maisie fought
The endless fight with all uncleanliness:
Beat hell out of the Indian carpets, turned
Parquet floors into ice-rinks, flayed stone steps
Already Whitsun-white. For dirtier dirt
She wore home-made fatigues: sackcloth apron,
Boots, a man's cap. 'Dressed like Sal Scratch,' they said.

She always promised me this clock that still
Fusses inside its Gothic wooden house
Of marquetry and glass. Pasted behind
The pendulum, in wilted gold on black,
The image of an eagle flying in
Delivering a field-marshal's baton
Over a muddle of trumpets, drums and flags.

Once, as a grammar schoolboy, Clever Dick,
I said to Maisie, 'If there wasn't such
A thing as dirt we'd have invented it.
What would some people do without it?' She,
Helping us out at home, my mother ill
In bed, thought this not worth replying to.
'There's not much in it, Maisie,' I said, shamed
As she came downstairs with my chamber pot.
'It makes no odds,' she said, expressionless.
'Needs emptying, a little or a lot.'

FIRST DAY

for Moelwyn Merchant

MYOPE, jackdaw-tongued, I was fetched to school
Too early. ('Only child. Needs company.')
School was an ark of slate and granite, beached
Between the allotments and the castle ditch.

Cased on the roof, the famous Hanging Bell:
Came, 1840, from the county gaol.
I'm 1917, from Old Hill, rigged out
In regulation infant gear: knitted

Green jersey, cords snagging both knees, new boots
With tags that locked my feet together. Hold
The tin mug with my cocoa money in.
A washed September morning, and the gas

Was on. Over the teacher's desk I saw
A cross made out of wood. Small steps led up,
But nobody was on it. Miss Treglown
Was writing down my name in a big book.

'Where's Jesus?' Without lifting up her head,
'Jesus is everywhere,' Miss Treglown said.
As if on cue, trapped in its rusted tower,
The Hanging Bell came to. Banged out the hour.

BRIDIE WILES

BRIDIE WILES, 2 Gas Court Lane,
Between the tanyard and the railway line,
About the time of the first Armistice
Scooped me, one Saturday, out of my pram.
Promised me the river.

My cousin Gwennie, nine,
And three foot eight to Bridie's five eleven
Said, 'You do
And I'll chuck you in too.
Anyway,
The water isn't deep enough today
To drown a frog in.'

'Nor is it,' Bridie said, sometimes
Quite sensible despite her role
As our local madwoman
Of Chaillot,
Making to bale me
Back into the pram,
If the wrong way round.

Decades on,
At Uncle Heber's Co-op funeral,
'I'll tell you something you don't know,'
Said Gwen.
'Between us, Bridie and me pulling
As if you were a Christmas cracker
We dropped you on your head.
I never told your mum. Or mine.
My God, but you went white!
We thought that you'd gone dead.

'Another thing.
It's always been a mystery to me
How you're the only one
Of our lot doing what you do.
The other day I read
That sort of thing can be set off
By a dint on the head.
Do you think that's true?
Perhaps you owe it all to Bridie and to me.'

I asked her what she meant by it and all.
'Not possible,' said cousin Gwen, 'to say.
Though Bridie may.'

GELIBOLU

THE PATH, under a thin scribble of pine,
Wavers towards a bay, a sudden shine
Of Turkish pebbles, sand, a banjo pier
Drowned in an evening sea: the scene as clear
As if painted on glass, and which would take
Only a breath, a syllable to break.

Across the strait a pharos flirts an eye.
Rough hills, smoothed to a sunset blackness, lie
Like children's cut-outs laid against the sky.
But this is savaged air. Is poisoned ground.
Unstilled, the dead, the living voices sound,
And now the night breaks open like a wound.

Gelibolu: the Turkish name for Gallipoli

I BELIEVE YOU WERE BORN IN ODESSA

NEVER having heard
The splash of a syllable
Or read as much as a comma
By my Russian friend,
I said as we walked
By the shaken fabric
Of a black sea,
'I believe you were born in Odessa.
Did you never see Chekhov?'

Squaring off his pince-nez
He replied, 'My mother once glimpsed
The back of him. A tall man
In a white linen suit,
White linen hat,
And carrying a cane.
Climbing the steps
Of a sea-front hotel.'

'Did he not say this?' I said.
    ' "It is very hard
    To describe the sea.
    But once I read
    What a schoolboy wrote.
    The sea is huge.
    Just that. No more.
    I think that is beautiful." '

Glancing at the silver egg
That was his watch,
'Time to return
To the Literature Conference,'
My friend remarked. A tall man
In a white linen suit,
White linen hat,
And carrying a cane.
Climbing the steps
Of a sea-front hotel.

CALICO

CALICO, ledged on the calico mountain,
Lodges in an empty pocket of silver
Over the sand-drenched plain, the Mojave
Forging its secret journey under
Sidewinder spiralling, sidewinder rattling,
Dusky heronsbill, desert-tea,
Flowering beavertail cactus, the sharpened
Bible spears of the Joshua tree.

Fresher than paint, the ghost of a ghost town
Takes its stand in the twelve-o'clock light:
Parking Lot, Ice Cream Parlor, Playhouse,
Schoolhouse dribbling the stars and stripes,
Repro guns and saddles and stetsons,
Rock shop, bottle shop, needlepoint store,
C & H Smelter, bath house, jail house,
Lil's Saloon and the Maggie Mine Tour.
Shadowless, the shadows wander
Broken adobe wall and stair.
Out of the canyon the poor-will startles
Like a bell the immaculate air.

And the Cornish were here, their names like
  granite
Scoured by a century of sun,
The vanished voices hymning to Zion,
Hollowed out by the accents of home.
I see Wheal Abraham, dark King Doniert's
Stone (which he raised for the good of his soul),
Tide-water sidling into Newlyn,
The weathercock swirling its gold on Paul.

AT ST HILARY

BETWEEN two Cornish seas, the spire,
Blazes the land, the waving air.

The dark stem of a Celtic cross
Sprouts, half-grown, from the shallow grass.

A tomb, exploded, shows the bones
Of a young sycamore. Slant stones

Cram the graveyard like ships stormbound.
A wasted urn drips shard and sand.

Like auguries, two seabirds lie
Motionless in the squalling sky.

Through rain and wind and risen snow
I come, as fifty years ago,

Drawn by I know not what, to sound
A fabled shore, unlost, unfound,

Where in the shadow of the sun
Past, present, future, wait as one.

Only the breathing ash speaks true.
Nothing is new. Nothing is new

As the sea slinks to where I stand
Between the water and the land.

BUFFALO

BUFFALO Jenkyn,
Five foot by three,
Came through the First War
Scatheless. Bullets
And shrapnel bounced
Off him, they said.

Skin, hair, clothes,
All buffalo-coloured.
Wore his head low.
Chest an escarpment
In the Rockies.
He'd have braked a riot.

Worked on the road-gang.
Shoved the trolley
And electric pole
With one hand,
Pasty and bottle of tea
Trapped in the other.

Face like a volcano.
After a day digging
Holes, raising poles,
Tended his allotment.
Moved about it
Like a mass priest.

Lived bottom of
Trelawny Street
With a slat-thin whippet.
Also two shiny cats that
Trailed him as if
He were St Jerome.

Bible, Koran, Bhagavad-Gita:
The Small Gardener.
Music, the noise of things
Growing. Today was at
Church for the first
And last time.

Leaves a hole
In the universe.
I see him making
The Fiddler's Bitch at 10:29,
Cut cabbage in one hand,
In the other, violets.

ARSHILE GORKY'S

The Artist and His Mother

THEY FACE us as if we were marksmen, eyes
Unblindfolded, quite without pathos, lives
Fragile as the rose-coloured light, as motes
Of winking Anatolian dust. But in
The landscape of the mind they stand as strong
As rock or water.
                                        The young boy with smudged
Annunciatory flowers tilts his head
A little sideways like a curious bird.
He wears, against his history's coming cold,
A velvet-collared coat, Armenian pants,
A pair of snub-nosed slippers. He is eight
Years old. His mother, hooded as a nun,
Rests shapeless, painted hands; her pinafore
A blank white canvas falling to the floor.

Locked in soft shapes of ochre, iron, peach,
Burnt gold of dandelion, their deep gaze
Is unaccusing, yet accusatory.
It is as if the child already sees
His dead mother beside him as they fled
Barefoot to starving Yerevan. And sees
His own death, self-invited, in the green
Of a new world, the painted visions now
Irrelevant, and arguments of line
Stilled by the death of love.
                                                        Abandoning
His miracle, he makes the last, long choice
Of one who can no longer stay to hear
Promises of the eye, the colour's voice.

MYTH

AND THE children, brother, sister,
From the mountainside returning

Saw at last their camp discovered
By the Morning Star Man. Saw him

Kill the cattle. Kill the people.
Kill the father. Kill the mother.

All the lovely people murdered.
For a while they sat among them

Their small words of comfort speaking
That the dead might hear their voices

As when living breath was with them.
The two children, sister, brother,

Seizing up a firestick journeyed
Over the red plain, the mountain

And the ever-swimming river
To the rim of a tall forest

And among the fern and flower
By a spring of silver water

Built a campfire, sat them down there;
Watched the sun bloody the ocean,

And above their heads a starshine
Printed in another fashion.

Suns and moons flew by like fireflies
As they lived alone, together.

'I want you as wife,' the boy said.
Said the girl, 'You are my brother.'

'We are as the forest creatures,'
Said the boy. 'Or those that wander

'The red plain. As free birds flying
The high blue. As fish that journey

'The long silences of water.
You shall be my wife,' the boy said.

And the sister and the brother
Lay and made a child together.

Made them children as the seasons
Flowed about them like a river.

And the children, men and women,
Wandering to nameless countries,

Made a speech from leaf and flower,
Made from ice and snow another,

Made a speech from mist and mountain,
From the sands a speech of fire.

'I have lost my spear for hunting,'
Said the brother. 'And must find it.'

Back they journeyed to the campground
By the spring of silver water.

Many men and many women
Walked that ground. And she was calling,

'Here your hunting spear is lying
Where we two first lay together.'

And the man came to the woman,
On her lips placed a soft finger.

'Speak,' he said. 'And I must kill you.
As the Morning Star Man. Kill you.'

Laid his cutting-stone beside her.

The principal source of 'Myth' is Roland Robinson's *Aboriginal Myths and Legends* (Sun Books, Melbourne, 1966)

SEDER

THE ROOM at first sight is a winter room:
The tablecloth a fresh snowfall ordered
With frail *matzot* that splinter at the touch
Like too-fine ice, the wine glasses of hard
Snow-crystal. To the shifting candle-flame,
Blood-glint of wine against the polished green
Of garlands, white of bitter herbs, and on

Its ritual dish the shankbone of the lamb.
A chair stands empty for the celebrant,
Unfree, who cannot celebrate; the wine
Poured for Elijah; the half *matzah* snugged
In a napkin for a young child to find.
The reading of the Haggadah begins.
Let those who are an hungered come and eat

With us. Those who are needy come and keep
The Passover with us. Though we dwell here
This year in exile and in bondage, next
Year we are free. Prayers in a mash of tongues.
Why does this night differ from other nights?
A boy is asked. Another at the door
Opens it that Elijah enters in

To blazon the Messiah, drink the wine
Of the unending promise, share the hope
Of Passover. Kisses, embraces as
The feast is ended. We disperse beneath
Uncounted stars as measureless as those
Children who marched into the wilderness.
Laughter. *Yom Tov. A Good Yom Tov*, they say,

This family, sometime traders in salt
In Novgorod: doctor, attorney, truck-
Driver, schoolteacher, mail-clerk, student, nurse;
The smiling grandparents, from whom God hid
His face, their eyes in shadow from the harsh
Rumour of yesterday. Every one
A trader still in necessary salt.

TWO FRENCH RENAISSANCE SONNETS

for Alan Clodd

I Sonnet to Icarus

Young Icarus, who fled earth for the sun,
Dwells here, audacious boy of courage bright,
Every true heart envious of his flight,
And here his body fell, its plumage gone.

Blest be the spirit that without dismay
Draws such advantage from so sharp a pain!
Blest the misfortune filled with such good gain
Granted a victory to his conquered day!

His spirit chanced the secret paths of air.
Strength may have failed, but ever his bold aim
Caused the frail stars to burn with brighter flame.

The sky his mark, his sepulchre the sea,
His death was high adventure. Can there be
A fate more glorious, or a tomb more fair?

after Philippe Desportes

II The Muses to the Poet

It was a day when winter's stubborn hand
Yielded, at long last, to the gentle spring
And field and meadow-pasture seemed to sing;
Green branch and blossom favoured all the land.

In rocky shade, beside a bending stream,
I lay in a sweet drowse, and in my dream
Before my sleeping eye a vision bright
Lit every shadow with its perfect light.

In company with Love, from Heaven's blue,
Each like to each as in a mirror's eye,
Nine Maids in shining circle round me drew.

They crowned my brow with myrtle, called my praise:
'Sing songs of love, sing love that cannot die
And you shall dwell with us in joy always.'

after Jean-Antoine de Baïf

A LITTLE STORY

TAKING, at last, the heart's advice
He walked towards the morning sea,
Felt its salt promise on his tongue,
For the first time in years was free.

The sun came up a richer red.
He saw it swallow up the dew;
Laughed as the white incredible stars
Still wavered in the risen blue.

To his surprise, the one he left
Declared an addled life and wrung
Desperate hands (so he was told)
And threatened self-destruction.

Indifferent, he journeyed on;
Tasted new wine and newer bread.
Tilled his own garden. Said, I feel
Somehow new-risen from the dead.

Reaching a tender fame, he seemed
As self-sufficient as the sun.
Safe in a tower of words he hid
His gradual wound from all but one

Who found, unsought, another love;
Untaught, another life to live,
While he who listened to the heart
Pondered on the alternative.

EMBRYOS

I

EMILY Dickinson
Called last night.
You are a poor cook,
She said. And look,
These windows
Need cleaning.
As for your poems,
Listen to me
A moment.

II

When I was sent at 10
To order a bag
Of coal (2/-),
Mr Fairbrother
Showed me the two saucer
Shapes he had made
In the floor
Standing at the same
Desk for 57 years
(Less the First War).
He wore them like
Medals.

III

Don't seem to dream
So much these days
About being Jackie Coogan,
My life as
Alexander the Great, or
The bulkhead imploding
In the Bay and the water
Spirting in. More often
I'm at the back of the Mixed
Infants, aged fifty-two,
The only one who can't
Get past G in
The alphabet.

WHY?

WHY DO you turn your head, Susanna,
And why do you swim your eye?
It's only the children on Bellman Street
Calling, *A penny for the guy!*

Why do you look away, Susanna,
As the children wheel him by?
It's only a dummy in an old top-hat
And a fancy jacket and tie.

Why do you take my hand, Susanna,
As the pointing flames jump high?
It's only a bundle of sacking and straw.
Nobody's going to die.

Why is your cheek so pale, Susanna,
As the whizzbangs flash and fly?
It's nothing but a rummage of paper and rag
Strapped to a stick you spy.

Why do you say you hear, Susanna,
The sound of a last, long sigh?
And why do you say it won't leave your head
No matter how hard you try?

Best let me take you home, Susanna.
Best on your bed to lie.
It's only a dummy in an old top-hat.
Nobody's going to die.

THE MYSTERY OF ST MYLOR

DATELESS, quite weightless, the Holy Boy
Hovers alone in frosty light,
His naked tomb fringed with the gold
Of winter furze and aconite.

His silver hand, his brazen foot
Are fire against a sky of slate
And now are flesh and bone, and by
A miracle, articulate.

Here it was the virgin earth
Opened her side where he might lie,
Drew a green field above his brow
Until his huntsman passed him by.

And neither fell the rain nor hail,
Nor ever spear of grass has grown,
And never a rag of snow that lay
Upon this roofless box of stone.

But when beside the famished sea
Prince Mylor lay as on a bed,
Silently his assassin came
And severed him his glittering head.

Plant your broad staff, Prince Mylor cried,
And it shall branch and it shall blow
And at its foot a root shall spring
And from that root a stream shall flow.

Tell me, I asked the Holy Boy,
The true mystery that you spell.
I leaned and listened for his voice.
It was the ringing of a bell.

LETTER TO W. S. GRAHAM

DEAR Sydney, or
Should I call
You Willie,
I don't know

Which. We only
Met once and
Didn't call each
Other anything.

Sitting here in
The thick bit
Of Cornwall
Watching the day

Move round my
Two cypress trees
I was thinking of
You and Nessie down

At the sharp end,
Enduring as usual
The first bite of
The Atlantic. I

Heard you were
Ill and hope
You're bettering.
One thing, your

Poetry was never
Under that sort
Of weather. I
Turn to it as to

A spring that has
Not failed me in
Forty years. In
Your fishbone

Tweed, silk
Stock and glass
Shoes you looked
To me like a

1st War Colonel
(Ret.) and not
The Wild Man
Of Madron I'd

Been warned to
Expect. But like
All poets, you were
In disguise; a

Good one, too;
Though when you
Said a few
Words on my

Behalf from the
Dead body
Of the Hall at
That reading I

Feared you might
Say something
Awful. Like. Or.
But it was O.

K. I thank you;
Think of you as
The Genuine Miracle
Working Icon

Man wandering
Starved and wind-
Scraped Zennor
Where the cows

If not the
Poets ate the
Bell-ropes.
The day I

Called with the
Fan from Germany
There was no reply
To doortaps and

You weren't in
The pub either.
Maybe you were
There all the

Time and took no
Notice. If so,
Fine. Noticing should
Be put to better

Uses. So continue
Listening for
The sound the land
Makes, the signals

The ocean sends, the
Secret speeches of
Air and fire as
You move about the

Scrubbed bracken,
The simple strong
Flowers, the written
And unwritten stones,

In the long fret of
The sea. You will always
Be there for me, always
Standing at the gate

Of Madron Black
Wood, a salt
Poem in your ever
Greenock hand.

SONG OF THE ONE WOUNDED BY WATER

I WANT to go down to the well,
I want to climb the walls of Granada,
to witness the heart entered
by the dark stab of the waters.

The wounded child was keening
beneath a crown of hoar-frost;
pools, cisterns and fountains
lifted their swords to the air.

Ah, such a tempest of love! Such a cutting edge!
Such nocturnal murmurings! Such a white death!
Such a wilderness of light submerging
the sands of the morning!

The child lay alone,
the city asleep in his throat.
A water-shoot from his dreams
fends off the sea-wrack's hunger.

The child and his agony, face to face,
were two green showers entwined.
The child was stretched on the ground,
his agony curved about him.

I want to go down to the well,
I want to die my death by small mouthfuls,
I want to cram my heart with moss,
to see the one wounded by water.

translated from the Spanish of Federico García Lorca

MOTHER AND CHILD

American Primitive

HOLDING in clear hands
The world's true light
She lifts its perfect flame
Against the night.

About its pulse of fire
Earth and seas run,
Season and moon and star,
The unruly sun.

Upon the hill a scuffed
Thinness of snow,
First of green thorn, a stream
Stopped in its flow.

She keeps within her hand
The careful day
Now the slow wound of night
Has bled away:

Vivid upon her tongue
Unspoken prayers
That she may not outlive
The life she bears.

PHOTOGRAPH

SHE WALKS among time-beaten stones
One hand upon the rood beam stair
That rises out of sticks and grass
Into a nothingness of air.

Here, where the abbey's great ship struck
And bramble bushes curve and sprout
She stands her granite-sprinkled ground
And stares the speering camera out.

She's dressed for Sunday: finest serge,
The high-necked blouse, a golden pin.
My grandmother: who sewed and scrubbed,
Cleaned out the church, took washing in.

Too soon, my mother said, too soon
The hands were white and washed to bone;
The seven children grown and gone,
And suddenly a life was done.

Today I stand where she once stood
And stranded arch and column sprawl,
Watching where still the ivy streams
In torrents down the abbey wall.

And still the many-noted rooks
About the tree-tops rail and run;
Still, at my feet, the celandine
Opens its gold star to the sun.

Firm as a figurehead she stands,
Sees with unsparing eye the thread
Of broken words within my hand
And will not turn away her head.

SAMUEL PALMER'S

Coming from Evening Church

THE heaven-reflecting, usual moon
Scarred by thin branches, flows between
The simple sky, its light half-gone,
The evening hills of risen green.
Safely below the mountain crest
A little clench of sheep holds fast.
The lean spire hovers like a mast
Over its hulk of leaves and moss
And those who, locked within a dream,
Make between church and cot their way
Beside the secret-springing stream
That turns towards an unknown sea;
And there is neither night nor day,
Sorrow nor pain, eternally.

DREAM POEM

I HAVE not seen this house before
Yet room for room I know it well:
A thudding clock upon the stair,
A mirror slanted on the wall.

A round-pane giving on the park.
Above the hearth a painted scene
Of winter huntsmen and the pack.
A table set with fruit and wine.

Here is a childhood book, long lost.
I turn its wasted pages through:
Every word I read shut fast
In a far tongue I do not know.

Out of a thinness in the air
I hear the turning of a key
And once again I turn to see
The one who will be standing there.

THE PRODIGAL SON

I COULD remember nothing of the village:
Only, at a sharp elbow in the lane
Between the train-station and the first cottage,
An August cornfield flowing down to meet me;
At its dry rim a spatter of scarlet poppies.

I had forgotten the cement-botched church,
The three spoilt bells my grandmother had christened
Crock, Kettle and Pan; the cider-sharp Devon voices,
The War Memorial with my uncle's name
Spelt wrongly, women in working black, black stockings,
White aprons, sober washing lines, my Bramley-
Cheeked aunt picking blackberries in her cap,
The butcher's cart, the baker's cart from Chudleigh,
From Christow, and the hard-lipped granite quarry
Coughing up regular dust under the skyline.

But this came later. I heard as I climbed
The white flint lane the still-insistent voices.
'Never go back,' they said. 'Never go back.'
This was before the fall of corn, the poppies.

Out of the sun's dazzle, somebody spoke my name.

SIBARD'S WELL

MY HOUSE, named for the Saxon spring,
Stands by the sour farmyard, the long-
Dry lip that once was Sibard's Well
Buried beneath a winding-stone
To stop the cattle falling in;
Yet underfoot is still the sound
At last of night, at first of day,
In country silences, a thin
Language of water through the clay.

At mornings, in small light, I hear
Churn-clink, the bucket handle fall.
An iron shirt, a sudden spear
Unprop themselves from the farm wall.
A voice, in a far, altered speech
Beneath my window seems to say,
'I too lived here. I too awoke
In quarter-light, when life's cold truth
Was all too clear. As clearly spoke.'

MOOR-HENS

LIVING by Bate's Pond, they
(Each spring and summer day)
Watched among reed and frond
The moor-hens prank and play.

Watched them dip and dive,
Watched them pass, re-pass,
Sputtering over the water
As if it were made of glass.

Watched them gallop the mud
Bobbing a tail, a head;
Under an April stream
Swimming with tails outspread.

Listened at night for a cry
Striking the sky like a stone;
The *kik! kik! kik!* of farewell
As they drifted south for the sun.

Whose are the children, and who
Are the children who lived by the pond,
Summer and spring year-long
When the clear sun shone?
Thirsty the stream, and dry;
Ah, and the house is gone.

RED

SCRABBLING for words, 'Don't do a thing,' I said,
'I wouldn't do.' And in that second, knew
From the lost look you gave, turning away,
We'd never meet again. Twenty years on,
I don't recall the detail of your face:
Only the coil of Easter flowers that lay
Crowning the moist hedge just above your head.
I saw the flowers there again today.

In storms, you were the rock we rested on,
Gave to the hopeless hope, tempered the mad,
Kept the worn faith when things were worse than bad;
Cast in the role of calm, consoling one
Persuaded us, because it was unspoken,
That ties of love, of blood could not be broken
And healed our loss, but never told your own
Until the day you journeyed off alone,
Checked in at some hotel, climbed the roof-stair,
Fell, with your secret, on the assenting air.

IN TWOS AND THREES

IN TWOS and threes they haunt
The shopping mall,
Child-faced, scrubbed clean, their gear
Theatrical.

The badges, red rosettes,
Ribbons they wear
Have an ineffably
Un-British air.

Tallies announce, in gold,
The ships they're from,
Speaking, as they do, in
An altered tongue.

They trade, each one with each,
A quarter-smile.
They find the rest of us
Invisible.

They look like children on
A wicked spree,
Each slung with parcels like
A Christmas tree,

Traditionally spending
All they've got
On creatures in some other
Blessed plot:

Another time, another
Place, for me
Adjudged as friend, adjudged
As enemy.

But Saturday was never made
For war
And they are on a dicky run
Ashore.

They do not fear the clock,
The travelling weather.
Are young. Are certain they
Will live for ever.

I LOVE THE LAUREL GREEN

After Etienne Jodelle

I LOVE the laurel green, whose verdant flame
Burns its bright victory on the winter day,
Calls to eternity its happy name
And neither time nor death shall wear away.

I love the holly tree with branches keen,
Each leaflet fringed with daggers sharp and small.
I love the ivy, too, winding its green,
Its ardent stem about the oak, the wall.

I love these three, whose living green and true
Is as unfailing as my love for you
Always by night and day whom I adore.

Yet the green wound that stays within me more
Is ever greener than these three shall be:
Laurel and ivy and the holly tree.

ST PROTUS & ST HYACINTH, BLISLAND

THE CHURCH, a stack of granite harvested
From Bodmin Moor, glints through uncovered trees
Above a valley loud with water, rocks,
Voices of bald-faced rooks that lurk and strut
High shelves of ash and sycamore. Beside

The porch the tilted ground is lit
With primrose, sharp-eyed daisy, daffodil.
The castor-oil plant gleams within a frame
Of window-stone, pure Georgian glass. Inside,
Along the nave, rough trunks of granite lean

Time-pressed this way, that way, in greying light.
Christ dies a gold death on the painted screen.
The altar glitters like a carousel.
The gilt tears of the Maries shine and fall.
Outside, a sudden pagan breeze, snow cool,

Flows from the waste of quoits and circled stones,
Roughens the grass skin of the goose-green where
Children shrill on the gibbet of a swing.
A boy in studded shirt and helmet revs
His bike up, circles endlessly the green

As though, for him, the day will never end.
Dark! Dark! the rooks warn. *Soon it will be dark!*
Unseen, an aircraft breaks the Cornish sky.
The two saints shudder on their granite plinth.
Pray for us, says Protus, says Hyacinth.

BIRTHDAY PHOTOGRAPH

AN EVENING sea swims in
To re-arrange the shore.
Swallows a thousand stones.
Comes back for more.

The young photographer
Sprints to high ground.
Stay there, he signals; moves
Half-circle round.

Draws with an easy care
In falling sun
Bead after bead, as though
He held a gun.

I stand, uncertain, on
A mince of shell and scree.
Tireless, behind my back
Hurls the long sea.

A talismanic Celt,
I fear, and I know why,
The thieving look that's in
The camera's eye.

From my house to the shore
Ten miles are spread.
All through the night the tide
Turns in my head.

Time, eager as the sea,
Dispatches one more day;
Lies, patient, at my side
And will not go away.

TRETHEVY QUOIT

SEA TO the north, the south.
At the moor's crown
Thin field, hard-won, turns on
The puzzle of stones.
Lying in dreamtime here
Knees dragged to chin,
With dagger, food and drink—
Who was that one?
None shall know, says bully blackbird.
None.

Field threaded with flowers
Cools in lost sun.
Under furze bank, yarrow
Sinks the drowned mine.
By spoil dump and bothy
Down the moor spine
Hear long-vanished voices
Falling again.
Now they are all gone, says bully blackbird.
All gone.

Hedgebirds loose on wild air
Their dole of song.
From churchtown the tractor
Stammers. Is dumb.
In the wilderness house
Of granite, thorn,
Ask where are those who came.
Ask why we come.
Home, says bully blackbird.
Where is home?

MORWENSTOW

WHERE do you come from, sea,
To the sharp Cornish shore,
Leaping up to the raven's crag?
    From Labrador.

Do you grow tired, sea?
Are you weary ever
When the storms burst over your head?
    Never.

Are you hard as a diamond, sea,
As iron, as oak?
Are you stronger than flint or steel?
    And the lightning stroke.

Ten thousand years and more, sea,
You have gobbled your fill,
Swallowing stone and slate!
    I am hungry still.

When will you rest, sea?
    When moon and sun
    Ride only fields of salt water
    And the land is gone.

ON THE EASTERN FRONT

To Helmut Pabst

HE LIES locked in a wood of winter snow.
The snow is blue, the shadows indigo.
If he could speak, I would not understand.
Ice seals the rifle to his silent hand.

A burst of snowflakes slithers from a fir,
Blunting the soldier's sight. He does not stir,
Nor does he speak, though what he says is clear
As the glass sky, the unforgiving air.

SPHINX AT SAQQARA

SAQQARA, and today I come again
Fifty years on, in Bible country, where
Cat-bodied, pharaoh-faced you hunker on
A spoil of stone, taking a little air.

A broken cobra on your brow, a flight
Of ruined wings, the beard clearly unsafe,
Paws more like boxing gloves, no wonder that
You're trying not to break into a laugh.

Unlike the Greeks, it never was your choice
To ask us the unanswerable, to censure
What, haltingly, we tell; rather, to voice
Unasked, in the heart's silences, an answer.

And still the face is unforgettable:
The unthreatening glance, the calm acceptance of
What can't be changed. *Patience, all will be well,*
You seem to say. *The price of love is love.*

The rapid sky burns down. Centuries pass
You as you lie in a small wilderness.
Steadfast, you smile, watch for the day devising
Its language of new light, the strict sun rising.

MY ENEMY

My enemy was the pork butcher's son.
I see him, head and shoulders over me,
Sphinx-faced, his cheeks the colour of lard, the eyes
Revolver-blue through Bunter spectacles.
When we lined up for five to nine at school
He'd get behind me, crumple up a fist,
Stone thumb between the first and second fingers;
Punch out a tune across my harp of ribs.

Ten years ahead of Chamberlain, I tried
Appeasement, with the same results: gave him
My lunch of bread and cheese, the Friday bun,
The Lucky Bags we bought at Maggie Snell's.
One Armistice I wept through the Two Minutes
Because my dad was killed in France (not true).
'Poor little sod, his father's dead,' my enemy
Observed, discreetly thumping me again.

I took the scholarship exam not for
The promise of Latin, Greek, but to escape
My enemy. The pork butcher's sharp son
Passed too, and I remember how my heart
Fell like a bucket down a summer well
The day Boss Ward read out our names. And how,
Quite unaccountably, the torment stopped
Once we were at the Grammar. We've not met

Since 1939, although I heard
How as a gunner in the long retreat
Hauling the piece from Burma, he was met
At the first village by naked kids with stones,
Placards reading 'Quit India.' After that,
Nothing; except our pair of sentences
To thirty years in chalk Siberias:
Which one of us is which hard to define
For children in the butcher's class, and mine.

SCENES FROM CHILDHOOD

for Stephen Spender

I MOTHERS' MEETING, 1921

THEY SIT like shelter-figures, folded, still,
On unrelenting chapel forms. Each wears
A second-best, straw-hat and hat-pin, hair
Done in a bun. Above me on the wall
A man with whiskers and a nightshirt on
Is seeing to some sheep. Floorbound, I sit
Beside a noisy fire. I'm sorting out
Old Christmas cards. My mother, my Aunt Gin
Are side by side. Somebody taps a bell.
The women bend forward a bit to pray.
Sing, *What a friend we have in Jesus.* Try
To keep awake while someone reads a tale
Out of a story-book. The tea comes round.
They pay their money in the Clothing Club.
And I remember how the women's hands
Are white and swollen from the washing-tub.
An hour, and it will be a world again
Of cleaning, cooking and the kitchen-range.
They know that things are never going to change.

II PARADISE

WE CALLED it Paradise: a plat of grass,
Strong weeds and wildflowers out of sight between
The broken guard-tower and the precipice
Of steps that fell down from the keep. The green
Grew higher than a child. Nobody knew
How it had got its name. To walk into
Its secrecy was to be lost from view
To all but God or some mad creature who
Had climbed the ivy to the castle top
And speer what the rest of the world could not.
See you in Paradise, we'd say. For here
Was entrance to another land, and if
No one had followed or had gone before
Its stillness was companion enough.

Today I saw it on the Castle Plan:
Close-trimmed and labelled, innocence quite gone.
Quite gone? From a washed sky the sun burned red
On green. *See you in Paradise*, I said.

III LORD MAYOR OF LONDON

'LORD Mayor of London,'
      the travelling woman said.
'Plain in the plan of his face,
      the cut of his head.'
She stood at the kitchen door
      in the sound of the sun.
I was wearing a frock. I was eating
      my Cornish thumb.

I think I was three. I remember
    the cartwheel hat,
the gold at her ear, the shawl
    with fringes that clacked,
the basket of pegs and pins
    fetched at her hip.
'Lord Mayor of London,' she said,
    'for that man-chip.'

My mother, bent at the stove,
    lifted her head.
She was censing the air with saffron,
    span-new bread.
Sheer with my three-year eye
    far off I could see
a somewhere of water and stone
    waiting for me.

Fifty years downstream, the day
    become other,
I turn in the river's track
    to discover
no more in my wake than a small-
    holding of verse.
'Be thankful,' my mother said. 'Things
    might have been worse.'

The prophecy long ago
    having grown thin,
did she buy from the traveller
    clothes-peg and pin
the day that my fortune
    was riddled and read?
Never a word
    my mother said.

IV Stang Hunt

Waking, aged four, I heard under the steep
Window a hunting horn, a scat of tin
Trays, kitchen pans, sycamore whistles, hob-
Nails punishing the hill. In my nightshirt

I ran to where my mother, father drew
An inch of curtain back, the oil lamp thinned
To a wafer of light, half gold, half winking blue.
I caught a blare of torches. The rough song.

'Stang hunt. It means a man was wicked to
His family,' was what my father said.
Beneath my naked feet, unseen, unknown,
Trembled the first small shock of ice, of stone.

V Forbidden Games

A LIFETIME, and I see them still:
My aunt, my mother, silently
Held by the stove's unflinching eye
Inside the tall house scaled with slate.
The paper boy runs up the hill,
Cries, '*Echo!*' to the black-blown sky.
The tin clock on the kitchen shelf
Taps seven. And I am seven. And lie
Flat on the floor playing a game
Of *Snakes & Ladders* by myself.

Upstairs, my father in his bed,
Shadowed still by the German War,
A thin light burning at his head,
To me is no more than a name
That's also mine. I wonder what
The two women are waiting for.
My aunt puts down her library book.
My mother winds a bit of wool.
Each gives to each a blinded look.
'Your father's with the angels now.'
Which of them speaks I cannot tell.
And then I say to them, 'I know.'
And give the dice another throw.

WHEN I WAS 14

AFTER THE Workhouse concert, the stone hall
A mix of Lysol and washed slate, the boys
In penitential boots and jerseys, girls
In stubborn aprons, eyes of men and women
The eyes of those in a defeated country,
They brought their Singing Man to entertain us.
'To thank the Artistes,' said the Workhouse Master.

The Singing Man, bald as a pebble, fringe
Of stiff pale hair about the jaw, arranged
One hand from cheek to ear, drew a white bead
On the roof-beam; faltered a drift of song.
His fellows gazed at him, at us, delighted
At such madness, as we were too (though with
More circumspection). And the singer, grown

Too conscious, suddenly, of his wandering song
Pointed a judge's finger at himself,
Retreated, grinning, to our kind applause:
The song unended he had brought from field
And folk of childhood. All I now recall
Is richness offered in return for dross.
The memory of a certain wound; a song lost.

TAM SNOW

to Kaye Webb

WHO in the bleak wood
Barefoot, ice-fingered,
Runs to and fro?
Tam Snow.

Who, soft as a ghost,
Falls on our house to strike
Blow after blow?
Tam Snow.

Who with a touch of the hand
Stills the world's sound
In its flow?
Tam Snow.

Who holds to our side,
Though as friend or as foe
We never may know?
Tam Snow.

Who hides in the hedge
After thaw, waits for more
Of his kind to show?
Tam Snow.

Who is the guest
First we welcome, then
Long to see go?
Tam Snow.

KELLY WOOD

WALKING IN Kelly Wood, gathering words
Frail as spilt leaves, fine sticks of sentences,
Spirals of bracken from the fallen ground,
I listen for the silences of stone,
The stream's white voice, the indifference of birds.
Safe in my quiet house I lay them out
—Leaf, stick and bracken—in the hearth's cold
frame,
Strike steel on flint against the page of dark,
Wait patiently for the first spark. A flame.

FAMILY FEELING

MY UNCLE Alfred had the terrible temper.
Wrapped himself up in its invisible cloak.
When the mood was on his children crept from the kitchen.
It might have been mined. Not even the budgie spoke.

He was killed in the First World War in Mesopotamia.
His widow rejoiced, though she never wished him dead.
After three years a postcard arrived from Southampton.
'Coming home Tuesday. Alf,' was what it said.

His favourite flower he called the antimirrhinum.
Grew it instead of greens on the garden plot.
Didn't care much for children, though father of seven.
Owned in his lifetime nine dogs all called Spot.

At Carnival time he rode the milkman's pony.
Son of the Sheikh, a rifle across his knee.
Alf the joiner as Peary in cotton-wool snowstorms.
Secret in cocoa and feathers, an Indian Cree.

I recognised him once as the Shah of Persia.
My Auntie's front-room curtains gave him away.
'It's Uncle Alf!' I said, but his glance was granite.
'Mind your own business, nosey,' I heard him say.

I never knew just what it was that bugged him,
Or what kind of love a father's love could be.
One by one the children baled out of the homestead.
'You were too young when yours died,' they explained to me.

Today, walking through St Cyprian's churchyard
I saw where he lay in a box the dry colour of bone.
The grass was tamed and trimmed as if for a Sunday.
Seven antimirrhinums in a jar of stone.

IN 1933

I SEE the deep November street,
The crowd suddenly still beneath
The dark lurch of the Castle Keep
As though the evening held its breath
Before the bell-man's starting cry
And the first rocket hit the sky.

It was a children's land: a tower,
Ships, houses grumbling in low gear,
The stick-man stalking through the Square,
Paraffin torches slopping fire,
A child's heart too afraid to ask
Which was a face and which a mask.

I see the gold set-piece that read
'God Save Our Empire', as each head
In fireworks of the King and Queen
At the far end of Castle Green
Dribbled blue flame, began to sprout
Flowers of dark. Went slowly out.

I AM THE SONG

I AM THE song that sings the bird.
I am the leaf that grows the land.
I am the tide that moves the moon.
I am the stream that halts the sand.
I am the cloud that drives the storm.
I am the earth that lights the sun.
I am the fire that strikes the stone.
I am the clay that shapes the hand.
I am the word that speaks the man.

EDEN ROCK

THEY ARE waiting for me somewhere beyond Eden Rock:
My father, twenty-five, in the same suit
Of Genuine Irish Tweed, his terrier Jack
Still two years old and trembling at his feet.

My mother, twenty-three, in a sprigged dress
Drawn at the waist, ribbon in her straw hat,
Has spread the stiff white cloth over the grass.
Her hair, the colour of wheat, takes on the light.

She pours tea from a Thermos, the milk straight
From an old H.P. sauce bottle, a screw
Of paper for a cork; slowly sets out
The same three plates, the tin cups painted blue.

The sky whitens as if lit by three suns.
My mother shades her eyes and looks my way
Over the drifted stream. My father spins
A stone along the water. Leisurely,

They beckon to me from the other bank.
I hear them call, 'See where the stream-path is!
Crossing is not as hard as you might think.'

I had not thought that it would be like this.

INDEX OF FIRST LINES